The Tr

Kathy
Best of luck to
you in the future.
Bob Whipple
3/28/06

The Trust Factor

Advanced Leadership for Professionals

By Robert T. Whipple

Leadergrow, Inc., Rochester, NY 14468

Productivity Publications
Legal Department
3177 Latta Road #122
Rochester, NY 14612
585-392-3601

Leadergrow, Inc. books and tapes may be purchased at special quantity discounts for educational, business or promotional use. For information write:
Leadergrow, Inc.
Marketing Department
Telephone: 585-392-7763
E-mail: bwhipple@leadergrow.com

FIRST EDITION

ISBN 0-9729119-0-1

Table of Contents

Preface

Have you ever stopped to ask yourself seriously why some people have an easy time advancing while others, equally qualified, seem to struggle? I did. This curiosity was neither academic nor altruistic. I was convinced more knowledge would lead to greater personal success. Early in my career at a Fortune 100 company, I bonded with 6-8 other young professionals who had the same desire and we formed a study group on leadership. We met during lunch hour and did reading and studying at night.

This education began my lifelong fascination with leadership. I took dozens of classes and seminars, studied countless audio/video programs, and read extensively trying to find the "golden key" that would unlock the secret of leadership. This sponge-like behavior initially led to more confusion than clarity. There were so many theories. It seemed impossible to combine them into a bundle of knowledge to apply in the real world. I went on to hold several management and consulting jobs within the company, using each one as a living laboratory for how to build leadership capability. It was fun trying new concepts and learning from the miscues.

In the late eighties, I stepped away from line management and joined a group of internal consultants in Corporate Quality for a temporary assignment that was both fun and vital to my understanding of leadership. We trained leadership groups on a Quality Leadership Process. My focus was on leadership because that was my passion.

The first year, in addition to teaching, I took classes from several masters of that era, including both W. Edwards Deming and Dr. Joseph Juran, the two quality gurus who started the global quality revolution in Japan after WWII. Peter Block and many other consultants instructed me on empowerment, another hot topic of the day.

My mentor was the senior corporate executive in charge of manufacturing. He and I were fascinated by empowerment and discussed our theories often. We wanted to know more about fully engaging the workforce. There were dozens of empowerment efforts all over the company. They went under various names: Quality Circles, Empowerment Seminars, Team Building, Integrative Learning. Which ideas were most successful? Could we distill key concepts that could be applied everywhere?

We put out a request for groups that had found an effective pathway to empowerment to contact me. A personal visit to each of these teams provided insightful data, while exhausting the travel budget. In each area, the consultants and local management gave their input first. The techniques were identified along with their documented successes and further improvement opportunities. Then we talked to the workers for another perspective. In many cases the managers and consultants were out in left field but did not realize it.

One department made a huge effort toward an empowered state. They had a special room with large pie charts showing progress on the different thrusts toward empowerment. There were signs of the mission and vision all over the department. Posters indicated personal behaviors and the values of the organization. The entire management team was turned on and driving this program. The local manager and his consultant described the program with great pride.

The workers also had glowing reports at first, but after the manager and consultant went back to the office, the story began to change. Worker body language showed a lack of full commitment, so I kept probing. They held back quite a while until one person finally spoke up. “You want me to tell you what is really going on?” he asked. “We all think this is a crock of shit. The program looks nice and it sure is impressive. They tell us how they want to lead this place and it sounds really good. The only problem is, they tell us a thousand times a day by their actions, they don’t understand it and they, by damn, don’t know how to live it.”

That reaction occurred in an alarming number of cases. Occasionally there was an area where something different was going on: a real congruence between the view of the leaders and the rest of the organization. The air was electric with excitement.

People were fully engaged in the business and really turned on. With enough practice, you can identify if a group has the real thing five minutes after walking into a room. The difference between phony and genuine is that striking.

I studied the most successful groups, trying to identify what they did differently from others who were working just as hard but getting nowhere. Those doing it poorly were often moving away from the very thing they were pursuing.

Upon returning to line management as Division Manager, I had the opportunity to practice and hone the key concepts for the next decade in another living laboratory of leadership, this time armed with some new tools and ideas.

This book is a collection of practical ideas to help you advance in leadership. These concepts address leadership in manufacturing, service, sales, non-profit, or any other sector of the working world. You see them applied successfully wherever excellence prevails. They are presented concisely to allow quick access to core concepts.

The common denominator of excellent leadership is building and enhancing trust among people. You will read why outstanding leadership pivots on trust and learn ways to build a more trusting environment in your organization.

Although no magic bullet will instantly make you a great leader, this book will help you avoid key errors leaders often make. It will help you identify and manage your leadership style for optimum results, regardless of your current position. Following these principles will have significant impact on your career and the careers of those you lead.

Acknowledgments

I want to thank the people who helped make this book possible.

First are the hundreds of leaders I had the privilege of working with during my career. Each one taught me new dimensions of leadership that helped form the basis of this book. It would be imprudent to single out particular cohorts, even though some had more impact on my understanding than others. I'll just say "thanks" to all I have worked with who helped educate me by gently (usually) pointing out my development opportunities.

Several people reviewed early drafts of this work and were very helpful at guiding the content and style of the book. They were Steve Frangos, Bill Hamlin, Mary Burkhardt, Bill Whipple, Diane McCue, and Ted Steans.

The artwork for the cover and the Leadergrow Logo were produced by Blueline Studio of Secane, Pa. 610-532-1119.

Finally, this book was a collaborative effort between my wife Kay and myself. It would not be in print if not for her. My contribution was the content and hers was making it into a respectable publication. It was a labor of love for both of us. I express here my debt of gratitude for the multitude of hours she spent laboring over manuscripts and gently helping me understand how to organize and write a cohesive work of literature.

Introduction

Leadership exists wherever there are people. In the corporate culture, there are two levels of leadership: basic and advanced. These conform roughly to Abraham Maslow's hierarchy of needs, where basic hygiene needs must be satisfied before self-actualization needs can be met. (See Appendix B.)

Basic leadership ensures people do the right things, like establishing the organization's mission. The mission is a statement of *what* we are trying to accomplish. Leaders make sure people have the baseline skills, tools, and resources to meet business needs. Performance evaluation and feedback are part of basic leadership. Maintenance of all operational goals, rules, norms, and expectations are included in this level.

Basic Leadership is a requirement to sustain the organization, just as Maslow's lower levels (the need for food and shelter) sustain life itself. Without basic leadership, a state of anarchy and chaos will exist. It is necessary for minimal performance but not sufficient for excellence.

Advanced leadership is more interesting. The leader is focused on helping people contribute to their maximum potential. Here you find passion, striving to be the best. The mindset is focused on actually reaching seemingly impossible goals. Enthusiasm for the enterprise is pumping through the veins of everyone.

Establishment of the organization's values and vision are part of advanced leadership. Values define the rightness of actions, and vision is a statement of direction. Actions of the leader must be congruent with the vision and values at all times. The leader's role is to establish an environment of trust, where people feel safe pointing out inconsistencies. This creates an atmosphere that deals with problems in their infancy, reserving maximum energy for pursuit of the vision.

Although this book deals with both levels, the focus is advanced leadership. It presupposes a good grounding in basic leadership skills. Most courses and books on leadership focus on basic skills. These foundations are a prerequisite for advanced leadership.

The book is organized in two sections. The first deals with creating the right environment and establishing a framework for your business. This includes identification of values, vision, mission, behaviors, and a strategic plan for the organization. Also included are ways to assess your leadership capability and discussion of six key leadership dimensions: creating trust, style, communications, strength, outlook, and passion for performance. This defines a theoretical framework for outstanding leadership.

The second section puts these concepts into action. It covers the process to achieve rapid and lasting change, plus antidotes for typical leadership pitfalls. The change process is discussed from three perspectives: organizational structure, optimizing corporate culture, and developing people and teams. Finally, the challenge to mentor future generations of leaders is discussed.

SECTION ONE

Chapter 1 The Leader's Role

Leadership Defined: Laying the Foundation

There are thousands of definitions of leadership, each correct for its purpose but limited in scope. No one definition is broad enough to capture the breadth of leadership. The following attempt is the best one I have found. It came out of IBM in 1974, in an internal book titled "On Leadership," written by Carole Kismaric and Charles Mikoloycak.

> "Leadership is an invisible strand as mysterious as it is powerful, it pulls and it bonds. It is a catalyst that creates unity out of disorder. Yet it defies definition. No combination of talents can guarantee it. No process or training can create it where the spark does not exist.
>
> The qualities of Leadership are universal. They are found in the poor and the rich, the humble and the proud, the common man and the brilliant thinker; they are qualities that suggest paradox rather than pattern. But wherever they are found, Leadership makes things happen.
>
> The most precious and intangible quality of Leadership is trust – the confidence that the one who leads will act in the best interest of those who follow – the assurance that the leader will serve the group without sacrificing the rights of the individual.

> Leadership's imperative is a 'sense of rightness' – knowing when to advance and when to pause, when to criticize and when to praise, how to encourage others to excel. From the Leader's reserves of energy and optimism, followers draw strength. In the Leader's determination and self-confidence, they find inspiration.
>
> In its highest sense, Leadership is integrity. This command by conscience asserts itself more by commitment and example than by directive. Integrity recognizes external obligations, but it heeds the quiet voice within rather than the clamor without."

This definition captures some of the charisma and emotion of a leader, but does not describe what leaders do. Jim Collins, in "Good to Great," coined a new leadership term, "Level 5 Leaders," which begins to address this issue. Level 5 Leaders are fanatically driven to produce results, and they produce consistently superior results. Self-effacing and modest, these leaders are workers rather than showoffs. An example of Level 5 Leaders in action is the window/mirror analogy. Level 5 Leaders look out the window and attribute success to factors other than themselves. When things go poorly, however, they see the window as a mirror and blame themselves, taking full responsibility. In comparison, many CEOs, not Level 5 Leaders, often did just the opposite – they looked in the mirror taking credit for success, but looked out the window assigning blame for disappointing results to others.

This book will describe several characteristics of outstanding leadership.

Exceptional leaders consistently do certain things such as:

1. Build trust by reinforcing people who point out inconsistencies, and understand each interface is an opportunity to increase or decrease trust between people.

2. Connect well with people by being genuine and reading body language with accuracy. Approach people with humility and the feeling of being on the same level as partners in the enterprise.
3. Build a winning and inclusive culture. Create an exciting and uplifting work environment, where everyone feels part of the team.
4. Treat everyone the same way. Do not play favorites or allow inappropriate behavior. Be firm but fair.
5. Lead by example, often sacrificing personal comfort or gain to demonstrate commitment.
6. Listen well. Leave people with a sense of being understood, rather than just heard.
7. Negotiate and advocate effectively on behalf of all constituents without loss of credibility.
8. Demonstrate strong business acumen and sound decision-making skills. Be able to "sell" difficult or unpopular decisions based on credibility and strength.
9. Create a reinforcing culture, where people at all levels recognize and praise the efforts of others naturally without insulting them.
10. Communicate at the "gut" level rather than the "head" level, ensuring people internalize the message rather than just hear it.
11. Effectively diffuse explosive conditions and calm stressful situations. Reduce the need for damage control by preventing flare-ups.
12. Manage themselves and their own emotions well. View the art of effective leadership as a lifelong learning pursuit.
13. Generate passion and levels of engagement, where people become emotional stakeholders in the business.

14. Develop people to bring out their best. Consider "growing other leaders" as a high calling.
15. Reduce the credibility gap between organization layers. Excel at being able to interpret seemingly disparate points of view with credibility.
16. Build a safe environment where people have no fear of telling it as they see it, and reward people when they do so.
17. Challenge people to be their best, and refuse to accept less than the best people have to give.

These characteristics are described in more detail in Appendix A. Two levels of skill are identified for each characteristic. One is a minimum acceptable level for leaders and the second is the mastery level. This checklist can be used to characterize the skill level of leaders. It is intended to augment rather than replace other leadership measurement instruments.

The Impact of Leadership

With exceptional leadership, it is nearly impossible for an organization to fail. Eventually the unit will rise to stardom. The rationale is simple: outstanding leadership is rare and, when present, the sheer power unleashed by this person in the organization will allow it to easily out-flank competition by creating a sustainable competitive advantage.

Unfortunately, the converse is also true; an organization reporting to a poor leader is almost certain to fail. Only incredible luck or windfall can prevent it. The reason is the damage unwittingly done by this person to the soul of the organization. The lack of clear direction and poor morale mean no amount of cheerleading or other management techniques can bring this organization out of the mire. The stock exchange floor is littered with horror stories of how the actions of poor leaders have brought companies, and even whole industries, to their knees.

Most leaders are somewhere between these extremes. Imagine if you could improve your own leadership skills, along with the skills of those around you. The result would be incredible forward momentum in your organization. This would reinforce the good leadership and allow the recruitment and training of other outstanding leaders. All of a sudden, you would find yourself working in a more successful and rewarding organization.

The highest calling for a leader is to help groups move from one state of affairs to a better one. To illustrate, imagine two extremes. State A is an awful condition found in many institutions today. There is little trust and even a decent dialog is lacking. Workers are convinced Management is only there for personal gain. Management tries to convince workers they want to help the organization survive in the competitive jungle. They explain that draconian actions such as downsizing or wage freezes are honestly in the best long-term interest of everyone.

The workers do not buy this at all, and Management continues to self-destruct. Most attempts to make things better backfire, as the emotions of people spiral into further decline. When things get desperate, Management calls in the consultants with an improvement program, and the whole situation becomes fodder for another chapter in the Dilbert series. State A is common in work environments, and those who benefit from it most are the cartoonists.

State A	State B
Work is an unhappy and frustrating necessity. People hate their work experience and find it painful.	Work is very exciting and uplifting. People cherish the time they spend doing work and consider it a valuable and enjoyable life experience

→

I witnessed a vivid example of State A when soliciting a United Way pledge at a small manufacturing firm. I was in the office of a VP and overheard a public address announcement by the CEO. "Starting today nobody is allowed to work over the lunch break." I asked the VP what that was all about. He rolled his eyes and said, "Don't ask – you really don't want to know. It has to do with some people working extra and wanting us to pay for it." Continuing with the solicitation, we heard the CEO back on the bullhorn a couple minutes later. "Anybody who has trouble understanding my last message can come and see me in my office. I'll explain it to you." My blood ran cold. How could such an atmosphere exist in today's culture? Needless to say, I got no United Way contribution and left as soon as possible. That organization is in the process of going out of business. They have little chance to survive without a change in leadership because they are too far down the slide of morale decline.

Degradation of State A with Time

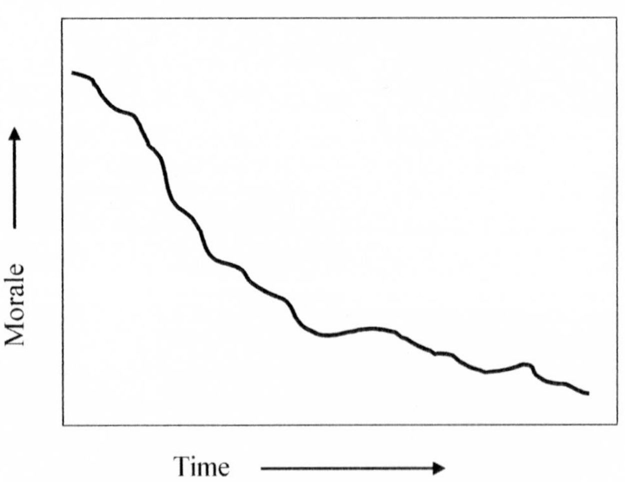

The degradation of State A increases over time. As rapport diminishes, attempts to set things right with quick fixes and new improvement programs only speed the downward momentum. It takes a complete catharsis to reverse the damage. That process can take years and usually involves changing the leadership and the entire environment. Often groups do not have the patience for this radical surgery, nor the courage to attempt it.

The real heartbreak of State A is its expense to the organization. Nothing works correctly, and much of the energy is spent on damage control. How can a business hope to be competitive in that state?

It is also expensive in human terms, as people stoop to unimaginable levels. Ordinarily honorable hardworking people intentionally harpoon a process because they cannot bear the hypocrisy they perceive in Management. In other situations, these people may be pillars of the community, church leaders, or loyal volunteers, but at work they undermine initiatives put forth by the current administration due to the atmosphere. The management process is perfectly designed to get the awful results being obtained. What a tragedy!

State B is stimulating to describe because it is more fun for everyone. It is that wonderful state where people are excited about their jobs. They respect their leaders and feel fully engaged in the success of the business as owners. They will sacrifice personal comfort, and even security, for the good of the entity. In State B you see people coming to work early and doing activities to help the venture in their time off. Any time there is a nasty assignment, there will be many volunteers to get it done. There is a state of joy and fun at work, as these energized people delight in beating the competition. Their focus is on the customer and competition, not each other or the administration.

Management is different in State B. They are mostly there in an advisory role, to support, reinforce, and mentor. Their most significant function is helping people get more of what they want through the success of the organization. They take on the teaching or coaching role as described by Wellins, Byham, and Wilson in "Empowered Teams":

> "At no time does the leader take on the problem personally. Instead by coaching individuals through the possible steps for handling the problem effectively, the leader offers help without taking responsibility for action. This is the soul of empowerment because it creates a sense of

> ownership. Out of habit, some team members want to give their problems to a leader to solve. Perhaps they lack the knowledge to solve the problem or do not have the confidence in their own ability to solve it. The effective leader helps individuals and teams look at their problems and determine appropriate alternatives. Employees will feel empowered only if they solve problems themselves. Most importantly, the next time a problem comes up, they will be better able to deal with it."

There is little need for the leader to discipline people in State B because most situations are resolved at the lowest level. Occasionally, a problem employee needs to be weeded out, but that has the full support of the others, since they are tired of carrying the troublemaker.

There is a sense of vision in these groups. They know where they are and where they are going. They set aggressive goals and often exceed them. They are also guided by a set of values that are more than a chart on the wall. Values have been instilled into the workforce through the actions (not words) of their leader. They understand "this is how we do things around here" and will not tolerate any deviations from the code of conduct. It is a kind of family atmosphere, but the kind of family that really supports and loves each other. Yes, in a State B environment the word "love" is often heard – in fact, that is one of the hallmarks of State B. It is hard to find words to express how deeply these people care about each other and what they are doing together.

The team reporting to Steven Frangos, author of "Team Zebra", was a perfect example moving from State A to State B. Their business was rapidly declining and morale was decimated. The prevailing attitude was, "Look at the facts. Our volumes are going down and we are closing factories. We are on a doomed ship." Through consistent application of exceptional leadership skills, Steve brought that group back into an award winning team in months, rather than years. Spending time with that group was refreshing; there was a sense of love and caring among the people that permeated the environment. They brought their business back to a healthy state and took on the challenges of a tough business situation with confidence and a sense of pride.

It was the same result Lou Holtz achieved several times as a collegiate football coach. He inherited six teams, all with losing records. Each of those teams went on to a bowl game by the second season at the latest. In his famous videotape on leadership, "Do Right," Holtz says, "The team came back, not because of a coach. They came back because the attitude was there." What he modestly fails to point out is that the attitude came from his philosophies and leadership. Without intervention of excellent leadership, the teams that experienced dramatic improvements under Lou Holtz would likely have gone on losing.

States A and B are two extremes. Most groups are somewhere in between. Unfortunately the average tends toward State A. If State A gets exponentially worse, State B is more linear, but it requires constant tending to avoid atrophy. This is the highest calling of the leader – to keep a finger on the pulse of the environment, to make small corrective actions whenever changes occur, and to relentlessly move groups toward State B. If this is the leader's prime focus, all other parameters of measurable success, profits, quality, morale, etc., will take care of themselves.

Corrective Actions move toward ideal state

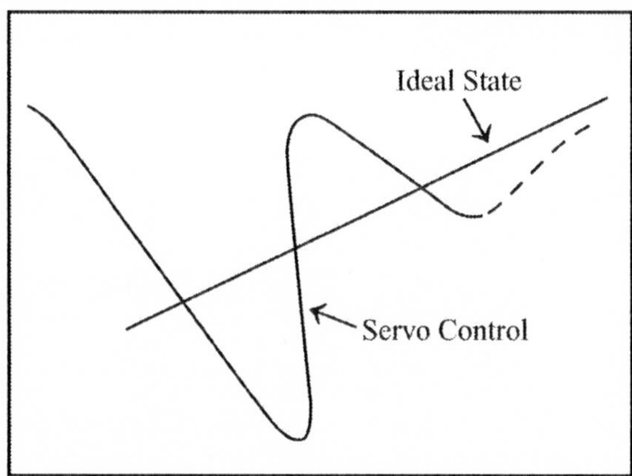

Fortunately, there is an automatic correction mechanism. It provides constant insight and a kind of servo control, a mechanism that works like the cruise control of a car, to keep things moving toward the ideal state as shown in the graphic above. This automatic correction means you must have an ideal state: a vision. Any time you are moving off the path, away from the vision, the control takes over, moving things back toward the ideal state. The next chapter will examine efficient ways to clarify and communicate the ideal state for your organization, leading to an efficient way to close the gap between current conditions and that vision.

Chapter 2 - Establishing the Right Environment

A company where the workforce is fully engaged is more competitive and successful. Achieving it requires more than giving inspiring speeches or hiring a consultant for training. It requires an organized approach and a multifaceted set of activities applied consistently over time. Some actions included in a typical improvement program include:

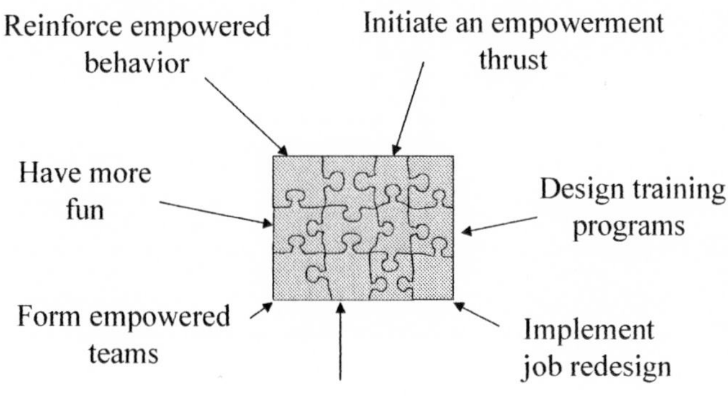

This kind of program is not simple, nor is it cheap. It requires investment and fortitude. The elements must fit together like a jigsaw puzzle to produce a state of higher engagement. Many leaders become sold on the idea that a set of programs like the ones above will be sufficient to move groups from State A to State B. ***However, there is a major problem here.***

Groups that approach engagement of the workforce with this kind of program often struggle. Many end up in failure because of mechanical implementation and the expectation that if you do these things you will automatically succeed. In my experience, it does not work that way. The leader must establish the right *environment* before attempting improvement programs like those above. The first step involves laying a firm foundation.

Just as children use wooden blocks to build the base of a tower, leaders and their teams can use the concepts in this chapter to build a foundation for their business. Some teams will start with a different color or shape block and their placement of them will be designed to fit their needs. As the foundation takes shape, the unique pattern of blocks begins to mold the organization and build stake in the edifice. While design creativity allows a nearly infinite pattern, it is paramount to realize there are universal forces, like gravity, that must be considered. For example, if the "customer focus" block is omitted from your foundation, you will most likely fail. It is critical to have a solid foundation, whatever the shape, and the blocks need to hold together to support the remaining structure or it will topple over.

The ideas presented here are building blocks that will significantly enhance the performance of any organization. They are presented in a stepwise sequence for clarity of understanding. It is important to avoid thinking of this as a cookbook approach to leadership. You and your team need to own the process and the sequence.

Working on Many Levels

Think of the following analysis in different tiers or levels. First there is you. You can do all the steps referring to yourself. For example, in thinking about customer needs, you personally have a set of "customers". You are a customer of yourself but your spouse and family are also customers. Your boss is a customer and so are your employees.

Next there is your immediate group. Customers may be those who buy your products, but higher management will also be a customer, as will other groups that interface with you.

Finally, the organization itself should be going through the same steps. For the entire enterprise, the customers will include outside consumers, but also others, such as the Board of Directors and the Stockholders.

Understand the level you are working on when going through the following steps, or you can become frustrated and confused. I will give examples to illustrate the difference. It may seem cumbersome at first, but soon the process will flow smoothly.

Step One: Start with Yourself and Take Responsibility

Griping about poor performance and blaming outside conditions or other people is a typical, but flawed, attitude of many leaders. The leader feels like a martyr doing everything possible under horrible conditions. The source of highest frustration for any leader is the feeling that "I could make this organization shine if it were not for the poor environment established at higher levels" or "If only we were not in this awful recession, we could have a better environment around here." There are hundreds of reasons why external things are causing problems. This attitude is nearly universal except in the case of Level 5 Leaders described by Jim Collins, as highlighted in Chapter 1.

There have been many true stories of high morale and empowerment in prison camps, where those in authority were beasts and the environment was stripped of all human dignity. It takes a special kind of leader to accomplish this, but it can be done. Stop blaming upper management or outside environmental issues and start making some positive changes *in your own domain* despite the challenging environment. Recognize things could be better and take personal responsibility for the current state. By focusing on your own behaviors and asking what can be done differently, a whole new approach emerges.

Note: the speed of doing the following steps is situational, depending on a number of factors. First, as a leader, are you new to the organization or are you a seasoned incumbent? If this is your first exposure, be cautious. Go slowly at first, and pick up speed as your knowledge increases. If you are a veteran at doing this kind of organizational work, you can move faster.

Another issue might be the level of urgency. If you have to make major changes over the next 18 months, it is quite different from being unable to meet the payroll next week. Be aggressive, but reasonable, in applying the following concepts.

Step Two: Analyze the Environment

Give yourself and your organization a thorough health checkup. For lasting change, exceptional leaders focus on their contribution to the current environment first. This process is difficult and extraordinary, which is why there are so few really great leaders. Chapter 3 has detailed information on using assessments.

Start by analyzing yourself as a leader. What is working and which areas need improvement? Identify your customers and assess their satisfaction with your leadership. Think about your strengths and weaknesses and write them down as a guide for improvement. What opportunities do you have to improve performance? What things may be holding you back, and how can you overcome these? Once this kind of grounding is complete, you can analyze the situation for your group.

Initial Group Analysis

Working at the group level, do some brainstorming with a diagonal slice of stakeholders, including employees, customers, suppliers, management, and peers. Determine what is working for your team, what is not working, and what can be done to change things. Be willing to hear things that are difficult to swallow. You may want to bring in a professional facilitator to help, but avoid the common mistake of hiring an outside consultant to go into the organization, do an analysis, and submit a report. The roles of the leader and facilitator are different. Do not delegate leadership activities to the facilitator.

As a leader, you and your entire team **own** the process. Be present and visible during the deliberations. A facilitator can help with the mechanical process, as with the SWOT analysis below, but must never appear to own the process. To get the real data, you must be involved in the acquisition yourself. Hear the issues and problems directly from the people impacted. Hiring an outside consultant to do this "dirty work" will start the process off on the wrong foot.

During these deliberations it is essential to suspend judgment, blame, analysis of cause, fear of retribution, and other conditions that could prevent the truth from surfacing. This may be tricky because if the current environment is one of fear and low trust, people will not feel safe opening up. Often it is necessary to have input given on anonymous surveys, or use some other means to get the true data.

SWOT Overview

After the health checkup, do a SWOT analysis (Strengths, Weaknesses, Opportunities and Threats) to understand the context of your business. This is one of many areas where an outside consultant can help facilitate the process. A person skilled in the analysis phase can lead groups through this critical step efficiently and objectively, preventing myopic thinking. A good consultant will not allow the team to delude themselves during the analysis phase. For example, if you claim your product is more appealing to men than product X, the consultant would ask what data you have to substantiate that statement. If you don't have it, you cannot claim the advantage until it has been measured.

The SWOT analysis starts with a thorough understanding of your customers. Who are they, and what needs do your products or services satisfy? Identify both internal and external customers. Where are they, and how do you communicate with them? What do they think about your products or services versus those of your competitors? Answer these questions, not only from your point of view, but more importantly, with data about how the customers really think. Often your internal view does not represent reality through the customer's eyes.

For example, a wholesale plumbing supply house was losing business, so they did an internal assessment of customer needs. They polled all the store clerks and management, generating the following four most important customer needs: ***lower prices, cleaner showrooms, more parking spaces, and better telephone skills for order takers.*** These seemed logical, so the owner developed a plan to address each deficiency.

Before plunging ahead (excuse the pun), he called in a research consultant to ask 20 typical customers about their plumbing supply needs. The consultant reported back that the plumbers mostly worked on contract at big job sites. They needed all the parts required for a job on hand before they could start work. Missing a single part among hundreds ordered could mean shutting down the entire job and losing income. With that background and a few more questions, the top three customer needs surfaced as: ***order accuracy, all parts delivered on time, and fast response if problems arose.*** Contrast the two lists. The internal customer needs assessment was wrong. The lesson is simple: never trust your own insight about customer needs. Always find a way to test your assumptions.

A second example comes from the airline industry. One airport had a rather long circuitous path from the gate to the baggage claim as shown in the "Airport #1" diagram. The passengers had to walk past the exit on their way to collect their bags. The airline detected some grumbling about this among the passengers and decided to put customer satisfaction first.

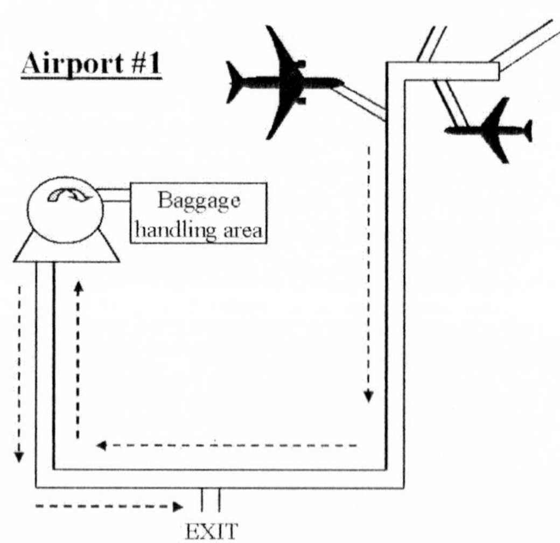

At some expense, they modified the layout to make a significantly improved passenger flow. (See "Airport #2.")

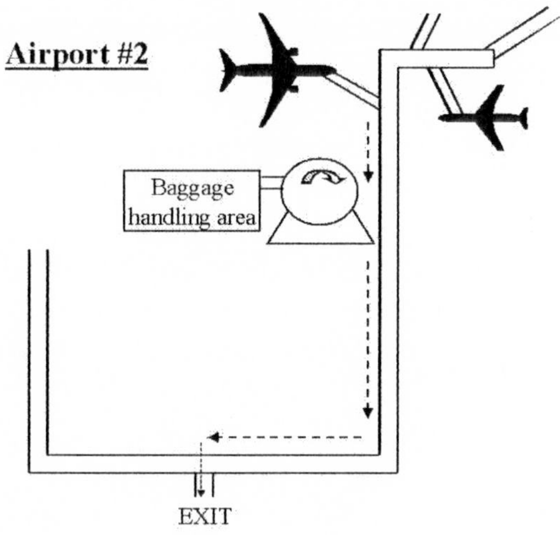

The airline executives were excited as they opened the new configuration. This was, after all, a huge step forward in customer satisfaction. However, in the following weeks, they experienced an unprecedented ***rise*** in customer complaints. Why? Because the airline had failed to take into account what goes on in the mind of the passenger. With Layout #2, passengers got off the plane and were immediately at the baggage claim area, where they had to wait for the bags to be unloaded. With the original layout, they had a chance to stretch their cramped legs, and by the time they reached the baggage claim area, the bags were already arriving. The ***perceived wait time*** was nil. Passengers equated this with better service. In the "improved" situation, passengers became agitated as they stood and waited for the bags. Even though by objective measures customer service had improved dramatically, people were less satisfied.

A final example demonstrates that often customers cannot articulate their own needs accurately. A very prestigious hotel in New York City ran a customer satisfaction program. Every hotel employee was taught to listen for customer input about needs and satisfaction. The maids and bellhops started picking up comments among the guests that the wait for an elevator was frustrating and long, since there were only two elevators in the hotel.

The hotel manager hired an architectural firm to come up with a solution. Could the elevators be staged differently or made faster in some way to provide greater customer satisfaction? After long study the manager was depressed to learn that their only solution was to install a third elevator at a cost of $1.8 million. However, this manager was very perceptive and creative. She came up with a solution for under $4,000. She simply had full-length mirrors installed next to the existing elevators on each floor. Guests would ring for the elevator and amuse themselves by checking their makeup or straightening their ties. As a result, they were less sensitive to the seconds ticking by and didn't notice any delay. The manager was solving a need by understanding her customers on a deeper level. It reminds me of the cosmetics executive who said, "In the Department Store we sell cosmetics, but the customer is buying hope." Only when the customer needs are fully understood can you assess the context of your existing business and begin to document the strengths and weaknesses of your group.

Strengths & Weaknesses

Identify areas where you have a competitive advantage over your competition. Scan all areas of the business, from research and new product development through collecting receivables and ongoing customer support. Take each area and identify where your group is strong or weak relative to others. To do this, you will need good data on the competition. This can be achieved by survey of customers, benchmarking or research. Many times, sales people on the front lines with the competition are a wealth of data. Most likely, your company has done a SWOT analysis for the whole company. The data from that should be included in your analysis because your group is part of the organization.

It is also important to include *potential* competition in this analysis, even if another firm is not currently operating in the market. Your network of suppliers is often a source of information on changes to the competitive landscape

Opportunities

The opportunities represent a creative approach to growing your business. Lay out everything you are doing and imagine what more could be done. Some of these ideas will be logical extensions of your current business, like selling milk through schools, as well as in the stores. Others might include ways of using excess capacity in a completely different market, like using an underutilized cereal press to make dog food. Use a creative brainstorming approach, where you go after as many ideas as possible, suspending all judgment to get ideas flowing. Opportunities are nearly infinite, so it is important to eventually channel these into a finite set of possibilities that make sense to do now.

Threats

Finally, document the threats that exist for every organization. It is easy to become defensive or go into denial in this phase. A good facilitator will ask probing questions and prevent missing a potentially debilitating threat. It is okay, even desirable, to act a little paranoid in this phase. If you have a successful business, there is a target on your back, and someone is aiming to reduce or eliminate your market share. To be successful in the long run, you must meet threats with countermeasures before they materialize. It is much easier to prevent would-be competitors from entering your market than to stop them once they have interfaced with your customers.

At this point, you have looked at yourself as a leader, the needs of the organization as a whole, and the role of your group. Note that the analysis between your local group and the larger organization often takes an iterative form. You lay out the issues at each level and see how they fit together. Ultimately, you have a deeper view of the issues, the problems, the need for change, and the opportunities at all levels.

This is a data-gathering process only. It will be tempting to make instant fixes to problems as they are described. Don't do it, even though that may frustrate some people. Explain that the assessment is vital background work for what is to come.

Resolution of problems needs to happen in the context of a whole new way of looking at things: a new vision. If you attempt to fix things on the spot, you run the risk of putting Band-Aids on cancerous tumors. Everyone involved will need some patience, and you need to explain the process up front to allow this. Having done this assessment, you can now chart your course in the proper context.

Step Three: Chart your Course

The next few steps involve understanding your values and constructing a vision for your group. You will weave these into a mission statement that identifies why your group exists. These activities form a framework for determining behaviors necessary for success. The key to building the right environment is acting consistent with the framework. Whenever someone believes you are not, they should be encouraged to speak up and be rewarded for doing so. This simple method is the most direct way to build an environment of trust.

But what if your Boss does not believe in all this?

It is frustrating for eager young professionals if their superiors place little faith in processes like these. Also, individual contributors with no formal supervisory control wonder how they can make a difference.

Do not press to organize the group above you unless your boss is genuinely enthusiastic about doing so. If that person is not interested in this approach, trying to pressure him into creating a trusting environment will backfire. This work must come from the heart.

The art of remedial training of one's boss is fraught with peril, so proceed with caution! Remember the old adage: "Never wrestle a pig – you get covered with mud and the pig loves it." That does not stop *you* from getting the benefits of a trusting environment in areas you control. You will be leading by example and demonstrating the caliber of your leadership to those above.

Every job has a leadership mode in some areas, even if there is no supervisory authority over people. If there is no group reporting to you, just document your beliefs about conduct in your current setting. Establishing a set of values, a vision, and congruent behaviors for your job will set you apart from those without that kind of grounding. You will be demonstrating leadership *potential.* It is important to start with yourself and not try to fix the rest of the world. As you conduct yourself in ways consistent with your personal framework, you will be rapidly propelled to a more formal leadership position.

As you improve your own areas of control, it may be possible, with the help of peers, to gently nudge your superior toward an environment of higher trust. The easiest way is to demonstrate the improved performance and atmosphere brought about by clarified values and vision in a few areas. Suggest the larger organization could benefit as well. Do not expect an overnight change in the boss. Instead, do the best you can with what you have. Understand this is a process, and patiently integrate it where the environment is accepting.

Step Four: Understand your Values

Values

The starting point is to understand your own bedrock beliefs and have your actions flow from them. Congruity is a central issue to good leadership. People will quickly notice every hypocritical action or statement. For example, if you claim "people are our most important asset" as a value, be prepared to defend all actions in light of that strong statement.

In "The Leader Manager," William Hitt describes the issue this way:

> "Consider the company that includes in its written statement of values that 'people are our most important resource' but behaves in such a manner to suggest that it is not truly committed to this value. The decisions and actions of upper management would strongly indicate that quarterly profits are the

> only real concern. When it comes to setting actual priorities, it is obvious that employees and their welfare are nowhere near the top. This blatant insincerity takes its toll on staff morale and voluntary turnover, and eventually, on productivity. Small wonder that in such companies, the major human relations problem is *lack of trust of upper management*."

Mahatma Gandhi was a perfect example of congruity. His strength was derived from understanding his values and giving up all the trappings of conventional power. His objective was not to fix everyone else; it was simply to live a life consistent with his beliefs and stubbornly refuse to back away from that commitment, whatever the cost. He ended up one of the most powerful leaders in history, having incredible influence on his nation and the world. He taught, "You must be the change you wish to see in the world." Transform yourself before attempting to influence others.

Start by creating a list of your deeply held values. These must be real beliefs and not just nice things to say, as they will be tested thousands of times. This first step is so critical, it is worth taking the time to do right. Get away from distractions while attempting to extract your core beliefs. The key is to examine yourself very carefully. You may want to work with a facilitator or group of friends on this, but start the process alone. Bring in others once you have a first draft to share.

Brainstorming is a helpful tool for this. Sit alone in a comfortable chair with eyes closed and some non-intrusive background music playing, and let your mind wander on the subject of your core beliefs. Write down anything that comes to mind, exactly as you think it, without trying to make it politically correct. Just capture the thoughts. This may be difficult to do honestly. This exercise can take from two to eight hours, and more than one try might be necessary. Once you are comfortable with the process, ideas will flow rapidly.

When it feels complete, put the list away and do not analyze it until later. Resist the temptation to charge ahead to the next step. Allow your subconscious mind time to work on the list. Additional items will flow naturally over the next week or so, when you are in a meeting, in the shower, driving, or even sleeping. This extremely valuable information must be captured. Keep a pad handy to jot down thoughts as they arise.

After a couple weeks, you should have captured 40-50 items, and the list will feel more complete. Start the winnowing process by doing an analysis of similar items. Write each item on a card, and arrange them into piles with common themes. Consolidate the piles down to a handful of key values. Four to six piles would be optimal, although you could have more. One pile might focus on your beliefs about what drives people, like: "I believe all people are basically good and want to do well" or "I believe people do their best work when they feel trusted." Whatever your cards say will dictate the piles. Next, give each pile a name. In our previous example, the name would be "what motivates people." Another pile might be "how to make our business prosper" or "what I want out of life." Let the data speak for itself.

Distill the input in each pile down to its essence and express it in a single phrase or sentence. This may be challenging or frustrating but it is an essential part of the process. Keep working the cards until you get to a handful of key concepts central to your beliefs as a leader. If there are private beliefs not helpful to share in a work setting, you can cull these out before sharing, but understand these are also keys to what drives you.

It is insightful to compare your values to those of the parent organization. They may not be exactly the same, but they must be compatible. If you have been dissatisfied or uncomfortable in your job, this exercise may help you understand why. You may be better off leaving to find a more compatible environment if the organization's values are not congruent with your own.

Now that you have clarified your values, let others reflect on them and do a similar process. Working with your team, repeat the same steps to construct a set of values for your group. Having done your personal homework ahead of time will make the process faster and easier.

The process of "wordsmithing" these lists can be frustrating. It is possible to have groups spend hours arguing over exact words for a values statement or a vision and get stuck on it every time it comes up. A professional facilitator can help streamline the process and avoid lengthy debate sessions.

If you are unanimous in spirit but hung up on words, get it roughly right and move forward. Use the 80/20 rule for this. (The 80/20 rule is derived from the "Pareto Principle," which states that in any grouping of items, 80% of the value will be contained in 20% of the items.) Focus energy on the 20% of items that contain 80% of the value and table the others. It is not the words that are important, but the spirit and understanding.

The final result should be a set of values fully supported by your key leaders that grew out of discussions of everyone's personal values. Putting this information on charts for the wall is helpful, but it is much more important to have it implanted in the minds and hearts of everyone. Only when internalized will it do any good. Communicating this information throughout the organization will be covered later in this chapter.

If you are not in a formal leadership position, documenting your personal values is still important. Use them to chart your personal course. Sharing them with others in your group or with your boss shows maturity and facilitates communication. One caution: this should be done with care and only when a proper rapport between people has developed. Sharing your personal values in the wrong way at the wrong time can backfire. It is better to weave the ideas into natural conversation than to force them on people. For example, you might say, "Let's allow Sally to provide her own wording for the proposal. I believe people become more engaged in the work if they have the personal freedom to choose how it is done. In fact that is one of my core values."

Step Five: Create your Vision

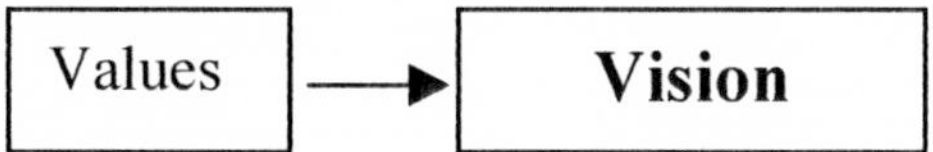

Without a well-defined vision, the organization has no true direction. It is like a ship without a rudder, sailing around at the mercy of the wind, hoping to find a safe port with little chance of reaching one. Creating vision is absolutely essential for any group because it gives a common direction and provides a focus for energy.

Not all vision statements are helpful. Some are relegated to plaques on the wall and ignored. This is a tragedy because an uninspiring vision breeds apathy and is worse than no vision at all. If people point to the vision statement on the wall and say, "that is where we are supposed to be going but they don't act that way," you are in trouble.

Joel Barker made videotape and wrote a book titled "The Power of Vision." I recommend it to all leaders who wish to generate a great vision. He presents four conditions necessary to create a powerful vision. According to Barker:

Good visions are:

1. Initiated by leaders – vision starts at the top.
2. Shared and supported by all – vision is supported by the "vision community."
3. Comprehensive and detailed – vision includes how, when, why, and what, so that everyone can see their part.
4. Positive and inspiring – vision has "reach" and is worth the effort.

If you close your eyes and envision the ideal future state for yourself and your area, what does it look like? This is a first glimpse at your vision for the organization. If you are not in a leadership position, your vision will be just for yourself. It is a powerful statement of your goals boiled down into a simple focused phrase. It should be inspiring enough to elicit your best, sustained efforts. If you are in a leadership position, spend some quality time with your team, identifying possible vision statements and weeding out all but one. Work on it with your key leaders. Get input from all stakeholders. It is critical for each person in the organization to make a connection with the vision, to own it. They must see themselves as partners in order to make it a sustainable reality.

This is not a 15-minute exercise. Some groups spend months working on developing a good vision statement. The process can get convoluted and burdensome if not handled correctly. If you are adept at facilitating group discussions, you may conduct this yourself. If not, a professional facilitator would be worth the investment. As the leader, even if you feel qualified to lead the discussion, you still may want to hire an outside person so you can become one of the people developing this material. The danger if you lead the discussion is that you could influence it too heavily.

In general, if a leader brings in a consultant to facilitate a discussion or to assist with a particular instrument or skill set, there is usually a high value. If the consultant is brought in to get into the trenches and do the dirty work of leadership, it is often a disaster because the consultant can undermine the leader. The leader calls in a consultant and says, "Things are a mess around here and I'm under a lot of pressure. Performance is horrible recently and morale is way down. I haven't time to fix the problem because I am overloaded just trying to run the business and I have to attend all these management meetings. I need you to assess what is wrong and recommend a program to get back on track. If my team buys into your recommendations, we will let you handle the program."

This leader probably has lost the ability to lead the organization effectively. As the consultant mucks around trying to understand problems, significant negative energy is unearthed but the consultant doesn't have the authority to fix these issues. Meanwhile, the leader is "busy running the business," and being micro-managed by superiors. Morale and performance go down even further until, finally, the leader is simply forced out.

This is why it is important for the leader to be the driving force in creating a vision for the organization. It cannot be delegated to a consultant or even a high-ranking lieutenant. The leader is responsible for making sure the vision statement is clear, compelling, memorable, actionable, and real.

Key ideas for developing a good vision statement:

- Most importantly, make sure your vision tells everyone where the organization is going. A nice sounding phrase that doesn't have pull makes a poor vision. For a football team "We will be number one in the league within 3 years" is a better vision than "We will improve our position in the rankings every year until we become the top team in the league."
- Avoid grandiose sweeping statements that are too broad. "We will become the best in the world at computer technology" would be too general and vast for a good vision statement. A better example might be "Our superior microchips will gain 90% market share with computer manufacturers in 5 years."
- Make sure people can connect their everyday activities to the vision. "Every interface is a chance to bestow great customer service" would allow everyone to view daily activities with customer service getting top billing.
- Keep it short and powerful. Avoid long lists of items that sound good but don't create a picture. For example, being "trustworthy, loyal, helpful, friendly, courteous, kind, obedient, cheerful, thrifty, brave, clean, and reverent" may be a good motto for the Boy Scouts, but it would make a terrible vision statement.
- Select colorful words that inspire rather than describe. "Our greeting cards melt the heart and transform the soul" would be superior to "Our greeting cards are better because they make people feel great."

- Keep it short. The fewer words the better. "Absolutely, positively overnight" is better than "Our packages are guaranteed to arrive by the next day or your money back."
- Use special words to emphasize your most significant point. "We will never, ever, run out of stock" is better than "We promise to keep our customers needs met by always having stock on hand."
- Don't try to be abstract or cute in order to grab attention. "We have the softest software in the nation" might be a slogan helpful on Madison Avenue, but it makes a lousy vision. Instead try "Software delivered on time, every time!"

The initial thoughts often contain the seeds of the eventual finished product. Craft these thoughts into words and images. Sometimes a picture or logo can be enough to communicate a vision, like the Rock of Gibraltar for Prudential Insurance. Other times, it can be a slogan, such as Wegmans Market's "Every day you get our best" or General Electric's "We bring good things to life." The expression needs to have "pull"; it must provide forward momentum.

Communicate the organization's values and vision to everyone in it. Do this well and often, as it forms the basis of everything to come. Frequently demonstrate your alignment with the vision by naturally working it into conversations. You might say, "Well, let's call the customer and tell them about this situation. After all, our vision is to put the customer first."

James Kouzes and Barry Posner state in "The Leadership Challenge":

> "In some ways, leaders live their lives backwards. They see pictures in their minds' eyes of what the results will look like even before they have started their projects, much as an architect draws a blueprint or an engineer builds a model. Their clear image of the future pulls them forward."

Some leaders are so busy they don't want to spend time doing this kind of work. That is a huge mistake. This cannot be delegated, and it is actually the most important thing the leader should be doing while restarting an enterprise. Being too preoccupied with the business to develop a clear vision shows the leader does not understand the power of vision.

As a leader, you need to make sure people understand your passion for the vision. Do this with both words and actions. Let people know you put your whole self behind the words.

Once when we were trying to instill a vision of significantly improved product quality, one of our parts failed to fit into our customer's equipment. They complained and we "fixed" the problem. Everyone pledged it would never happen again, but a similar problem recurred a couple years later because everyone did not follow the "fix." Somehow, people needed to get past the rhetoric about improving quality and realize a permanent improvement was required.

I wrote my resignation from the company without a date and put a copy in my desk drawer. I announced that the resignation would be pulled out, signed, dated and submitted the next time a part of ours failed to work in customer equipment. I told every group about the letter and even showed it to some people. Although not explicitly stated, most people extrapolated if the boss was to lose his job over poor quality, others would be similarly affected. We never had that kind of problem again. The vision sank in and registered.

Look at the policies and procedures of your organization and test them against the new vision. Often you will need to modify them to be consistent. Ignoring this step will result in confusion and lack of commitment to the vision.

Warren Bennis writes:

> "The only way a leader is going to translate vision into reality – an ability that is the essence of leadership – is to anchor and implement and execute that vision through a variety of policies, practices, procedures, and systems that will bring in people and empower them to implement the vision."

Translating the vision into a focus on current activities is the function of a mission statement.

Step Six: Create a Mission Statement

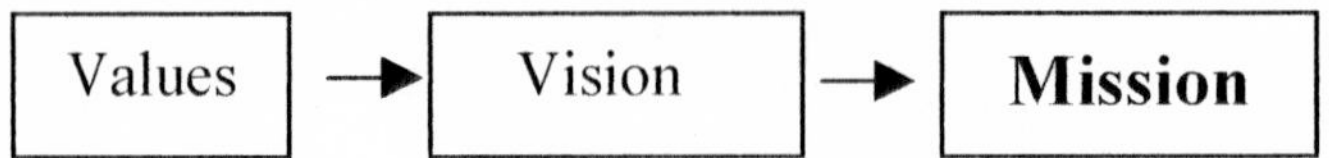

With the completion of your values and vision, people understand where they are going. These statements will be modified over time as necessary to keep them fresh and relevant. Having a mission statement to clarify and communicate why you exist helps integrate the previous work.

In his book, "Principle-Centered Leadership", Steven Covey explains it this way:

> "Most executives do not realize what is involved in creating a mission statement that truly represents deeply shared values and vision at all levels of the organization. It takes patience, a long-term perspective, and meaningful involvement – and few organizations rank high in those virtues. Many organizations have a mission statement, but typically people are not committed to it because they are not involved in developing it; consequently it is not part of the culture. Culture, by definition assumes shared vision and values, as represented by a mission statement put together and understood and implemented by all levels of the organization."

A good mission statement is important because it lets everyone know what he or she is supposed to be doing now to move toward the vision. If your mission was to win more than 80% of your games in pursuit of a vision to be the best rugby team in North America in 2 years, you would be hard pressed to support singing lessons for all players. The mission helps you test the sanity of proposed actions. Is this action really supporting the mission?

Constructing a mission statement is a team effort similar to the final phases of the vision work, but with a different focus. The mission statement is focused on today. It clarifies what you are doing now, while the vision statement is focused on the future. For example, if your completed mission statement begins with "Our mission is to become…." (a typical wording), you are mixing the concepts of mission and vision.

Usually, the mission is derived from a list of brainstorm items obtained in a group session. Once everyone has an opportunity to express their opinions, the group can have a pithy discussion on forging an operative, non-ambiguous mission statement. It is fine for a mission statement to contain a few key bullets, but avoid a long shopping list. The mission is there to provide focus. If the end product has more than four items, it should be challenged. For example, a good mission statement is provided by Southwest Airlines. "The mission of Southwest Airlines is dedication to the highest quality of customer service delivered with a sense of warmth, friendliness, individual pride, and company spirit."

The mission forms a basis for the strategic plan that will be developed in Step Nine. As a thumbnail version of the strategic plan, it helps people recognize how their actions lead to accomplishing the plan. Developing the mission statement and strategic plan is an iterative process that bounces back and forth until both are consistent and lead to the vision.

For people not in formal leadership roles, the mission statement is just as important. It allows you to test the validity of current actions. If your actions often deviate from the mission, it's time to revisit what you are doing. Something is out of kilter.

Step Seven: Agree on Team Behaviors

Many groups find it helpful to construct a list of behaviors to go with the values, vision, and mission. This is a set of statements defining how we treat each other and how we conduct ourselves. Construct these with the same care as the values, vision, and mission. They also form the bedrock to test against. Although the values exercise starts with the leader alone, the statement of expected behaviors needs to be a group process from the outset. Having agreement with the majority of people is crucial. If you are not in a leadership position the list of behaviors will be for yourself.

There are literally hundreds of things you could put on this list, but it is better kept short. You can always modify it later if there are glaring omissions. There are no right or wrong items as long as there is solidarity to do what is listed. Attitude is the key. This is not a legalistic set of rules to enslave, but a pact the team agrees to follow.

To illustrate, this list of behaviors was created by one of my teams and worked well for many years:

- When in conflict we will try to see the situation from the other's perspective.
- We will not leave a meeting with a "silent no" – we will commit together.
- We will listen to each other but not beat dead horses (80/20 rule.)
- We will build an environment of trust.
- We will work together on a finite number of common goals.
- We will be more inclined to ask for and offer help.

Your list should reflect your own needs and vision.

At this point, you have clarified your beliefs. You know why you exist, where you are going, and how you will treat each other. This is a framework by which you can test all actions in the future and the foundation that enables the growth of trust.

Step Eight: Create an Environment of Trust

Now you can begin to create an environment of trust. This will be the basis for the business to grow and prosper. Values, vision, behaviors, and trust are the heart of leadership. As Bennis noted, "You start with a vision. You build trust. And you create meaning. A leader creates meaning by creating an environment where people are reminded of what is important."

The central idea behind good leadership is to become a model of consistency, demonstrating the values, vision and behaviors, while continually executing the plan. When people do not live by these concepts, regardless of position, they are moving the team away from the vision and need to leave. In a speech to his managers at Boca Raton, Jack Welch of General Electric gave a compelling example of this:

> "Look around you. There are five fewer officers here than there were last year. One was removed for the numbers, and four were asked to leave because they did not practice our values.
>
> The reason for taking so much time on this is that it's important. We can't be talking about reality, candor, globalization, boundary-less, speed, and empowerment and have people who don't embrace these values. Everyone must walk the talk."

If you are successful at building trust, everything else will be easier. If you are not, expect to struggle in all areas, regardless of effort. Gaining and maintaining trust is a major challenge for any leader or any employee who wants to advance. Chapter 4 addresses methods for building an environment of trust in your organization.

Step Nine: Develop a Strategic Plan

Having a philosophical framework in place is a good start, but you also need a detailed plan for moving forward. The plan will include the most important business drivers for your organization, how you intend to measure and improve them, along with the needed strategies and tactics. For non-leaders, the plan will constitute a personal map for improvement.

Start by identifying the key drivers for your organization. These are things that, if done well, will propel your business toward the vision. Customer satisfaction is a key driver for most businesses, as is profitability. Others may include things like quality improvement and improving cycle time. Develop a handful of key drivers. If the list is too long, it will confuse rather than focus. I will use an example of a typical key driver, "improving profitability," to demonstrate the process of creating a strategic plan.

Identify how you will measure progress in each of the key driver areas. Measuring things is crucial for forward momentum. The old adage, "what gets measured, gets done," is literally true. Strive to identify 2-3 ways to measure each key driver area from differing angles. The measure provides a focus for energy and also data on which successes can be noted and reinforced. Possible measures for our current example might be "manufacturing margin" (revenue minus cost of goods sold) and "return on investment" (revenue divided by total investments.) These can be plotted against short-term and long-term goals to identify progress and celebrate it when appropriate.

Now identify improvement opportunities. These will be ways to make each measure move in the desired direction. For this example, you might identify a productivity improvement program in manufacturing or a new advertising campaign to increase sales. Each measure should have a few improvement opportunities that will drive progress.

You are now in a position to document strategies required to accomplish these improvements and to identify specific tactics. In our example, you might identify a strategy to engage in a Lean Manufacturing program to improve margins. The next step would be to identify associated tactics, such as hiring a consultant, training all employees in lean concepts, instituting a new reward system based on implementation of lean principles, etc. You may have several strategies and dozens of tactics for each key driver. Finally, you make the commitment and begin executing your plan.

Below is a table outlining the example we have been citing. The same pattern must be developed for all your key drivers. Assess the relative priorities of these so there is a cohesive plan consistent with the vision in the event of resource constraints. A plan that is well documented, internalized, supported, and communicated will drive the business rapidly toward the vision. It also lets people know what to do and, more importantly, what not to do. It provides a roadmap for focused effort.

Typical Strategic Plan

Step Ten: Empower Change and Excellence

Having established the values, vision, mission, behaviors, and strategic plan for the organization, with special focus on building trust, you have a firm foundation. You have created an environment where the improvement activities at the start of this section can have a huge impact. Not doing these steps first means the efforts will fall on barren ground. The next chapter outlines methods to get started on the process just described. To begin, you need an accurate view of your effectiveness as a leader.

Chapter 3 - Assessing Key Elements of Excellent Leadership

How do you assess the quality of your leadership? All leaders operate with a blind spot. Even if someone secretly videotaped you for a full day, you would not get an accurate picture of how others perceive your style.

The paradox is, nothing is more important to successful leadership than how others react to you. Resolving this dichotomy requires the ability to absorb all forms of input and an environment where people feel safe sharing their feelings. A trusting atmosphere can form the surface of an incredible mirror, allowing you to see yourself for the first time as others do. This breaks the paradox and allows true growth in leadership capability.

Chapter 4 deals with creating the kind of environment where people speak their mind, allowing leaders to assess themselves. This chapter deals with the other forms of leadership assessments.

Look at the Results

Looking at results is a great way to measure your leadership ability, but the bottom line is not the only indicator because performance is situational. A mediocre leader can do very well in a high growth area or a superb leader can struggle to make a turn-around in a bad situation.

Plot your group's results against the goals set by the organization. If you rarely make the grade, it is a leadership failure. Ask yourself what must change. Even if you are meeting goals, there still may be leadership issues. Often leaders can do well in the short term by browbeating people and creating an environment of fear. The results may look impressive for a while, but they will not be sustained.

Use Assessment Instruments

There are many instruments that can help measure the quality of your leadership. Many of these also allow comparison of your capability to statistically valid groups of similar leaders.

A good example is the Leadership Assessment Inventory in Appendix A of "The Leader Manager," by William D. Hitt. This instrument contains 100 questions broken down into 10 major categories, with 10 questions in each.

Question categories are:

1. Personal attributes
2. The leader as a change agent
3. Creating the vision
4. Developing the Team
5. Clarifying the values
6. Positioning
7. Communication
8. Empowering
9. Coaching
10. Measuring

The instrument allows you to profile strengths and weaknesses, creating a focused improvement plan. This is a simple and helpful tool to track your progress over the years. Use it annually with your group and keep a history of your improvement efforts. If you can achieve a well-balanced high score on this test, you are doing well as a leader.

Another tool is the Leadership Practices Inventory described in Appendix B of "The Leadership Challenge" by James M. Kouzes and Barry Z. Posner. For more information on this instrument contact University Associates, 8517 Production Avenue, San Diego California 92121, (619) 578-5900.

Leaders are measured along five dimensions:

1. Challenging the process
2. Inspiring a shared vision
3. Enabling others to act
4. Modeling the way
5. Encouraging the heart

This inventory allows you to compare your own profile to a statistically valid profile of other leaders. It is most valuable for understanding your rank versus a broader population across the country. It is less useful for trend data, since the population moves very slowly over time.

There are numerous surveys available on the Internet and in leadership books. Most large companies develop their own internal instruments, supporting their vision and values. These are mandated surveys that often impact pay treatment. Unfortunately, there are many drawbacks to linking leadership surveys directly to compensation.

Drawbacks to having pay link directly to leadership surveys:

- Skewed samples – Sometimes the sample is random; sometimes it is skewed to reflect some particular demographic. The sample also depends on whether the rated individual or the supervisor is selecting the raters.

- Great leader in a tough spot – This sometimes happens when a high potential leader is given a "killer" assignment. Ratings often will look bad compared to history, especially during the first year. Many leaders have been brought down or lost confidence because a short-term assignment made them look bad.

- Not accounting for risk – Sometimes situations call for leaders to do risky things, trying to turn situations around. That can have a negative impact on short-term results.

- Revenge - People sometimes intentionally trash the data due to a personal vendetta. An individual might rate a leader extremely low on all dimensions, just to lower the average score. With a small sample size typical of surveys, this can give a very distorted picture. Since good leaders are sometimes unpopular with constituents as discussed in Chapter 7, this problem is common.

- Tampering - Since each leader knows the questions in advance, some will waste time and energy "campaigning" for good ratings. During rating periods, this artful politicking deflects energy away from more important topics. It often resembles a game to win rather than a helpful assessment.

- Competition and ill-will – Leadership surveys can pit one leader against another if pay is strictly divided according to survey results. Leaders may undermine the efforts of parallel groups, so they will look better by comparison. These political maneuvers are often so subtle that nobody, including the perpetrator, are even aware of them.

To avoid these problems, use surveys as only one indicator of a leader's performance and consider the circumstances.

As an employee, if you believe an evaluation of your leadership is not correct, it becomes a delicate issue between you and your supervisor. Avoid trying to discredit the data or it will sound like sour grapes and be heavily discounted. A better approach is to have open discussions with raters (if you know who they are) about their observations. Do this with maturity and you can glean more data, along with a specification for improving ratings next year. Attacking the survey or methods will generally backfire and label you as a complainer. It won't help your cause.

Many surveys are done "blind", such that the rated leader has no idea who provided the data. In this case, you have no choice but to review the input carefully with your superior. Try to provide ballast to skewed input with historical data of your own.

DO NOT generate new data using the same survey on a different population. Even if you do this with highest integrity, it will smack of manipulation and do you more harm than good.

Often instruments are applied in a 360-degree view of the leader. The superiors, peers, and subordinates of a leader, in addition to the leader himself, measure capabilities. The juxtaposition of these data provides good insight. However, the 360-degree technique has many potential pitfalls as well and needs to be designed and administered by a competent practitioner or serious side effects like the ones above can occur. This is another example of where a good consultant or HR expert can help.

Drawbacks to doing 360-Degree Assessments Every Year

Incomplete

Whether a 360-degree leadership survey is administered by a consultant or is simply a routine procedure, it is important to keep these data in proper perspective. Evaluations are helpful tools, but they don't tell a complete story. They should not be the only factor used to measure the effectiveness of a leader. Take the long-term track record into account, as well as the nature of the current assignment. Pay attention to what people say about a leader's ability not just what the survey numbers indicate. Often they paint entirely different pictures. If you get differing views depending on the data gathering method, add more study before pigeon-holing someone into a "marginal leader" slot.

Less Useful over Time

For a while, I collected assessment tools like a philatelist would stamps. Each instrument was helpful at providing insight, but after a while they all started to sound the same. Using the same instrument for several years enables historical comparison, but provides less insight over time because eventually repetition will cause people to respond mechanically. When the validity of historical comparison becomes compromised, it is time to change to a different instrument.

Limited in Scope

Most surveys focus on how well the leader champions the values of the organization and the results this person delivers against tough goals. They ask whether the leader created a compelling vision for the organization and followed the cookbook of leadership "things to do." Although all these are critical elements of leadership, the surveys often miss the real essence of leadership.

Questions that Get to the Essence of Leadership

For about 2 years, with the help of my key leaders, I compiled a list of concepts observed in our laboratory of leadership. No concept was very profound by itself, but collectively they gave a different view of the dimensions of great leadership. Some were unique perspectives not seen elsewhere. We distilled each item into a question format. Here are a few questions from the list.

Do people tell you they admire your backbone?

Do you ever bribe your people? Is that good leadership?

Do you often make people angry? Is that good leadership?

When things go terribly wrong are you depressed or energized?

Do people do things they know you wouldn't approve of behind your back?

Are people sometimes afraid of you? Is that good or bad leadership?

Do your reinforcement efforts ever backfire?

Do people accuse you of overreacting or would they more likely call you very demanding?

Are you able to keep from getting mired down in bureaucratic mumbo jumbo without annoying the powers that be?

Are there several "folk tales" about particularly outrageous deeds you have done (good or bad?)

When you approach a small group of workers does their body language change?

Do you find out troubling things others have said about you secondhand?

Is your team pushing you to revise their goals upward?

Are you an abstract communicator or a gut level communicator?

What is the average time for you to return a phone call or e-mail?

When making group presentations, do you ever find people's eyes glazing over?

We collected a couple hundred questions and boiled them down by combination and elimination. Finally, we sorted them into piles of like subject matter and gave each pile a name. The following six areas emerged.

The essence of leadership:

Trust	Strength and Courage
Communication	Outlook
Style	Passion

The insight gleaned from this exercise was particularly helpful. For example, style is something normally dealt with on a "take it or leave it" basis in most leadership training: identify your style and that of others, then modify behaviors to reduce friction and work better together. Rarely will you find insights dealing with how to *modify or manage* your style, yet this has great potential for creating stronger leaders.

Chapters 4 - 7 examine the key leadership characteristics (trust, communication, style, strength, outlook and passion) in detail and investigate how you can grow as a leader and grow other leaders on each dimension.

Chapter 4 - Creating an Environment of Trust

Trust is the Key

Trust is the key to good leadership because, with an environment of trust, the organization can survive any kind of emotional or business problem and emerge stronger. It also allows the maximum energy to be directed at pursuing the vision, rather than engaging in political games or damage control.

The ability to challenge without fear is the key to building an environment of trust. Warren Bennis said: "Learn how to generate and sustain trust. To do this, reward people for disagreeing, reward innovation, and tolerate failure. If you are an effective leader, what you say is congruent with what you do." I call this atmosphere a "real" environment.

Joan was a leader who had been with a department about 8 months. I asked if she thought an environment of trust had developed in her new assignment. She said, "For the most part, yes, but some people are still playing games with me." The concept of people playing games to outwit each other is an insightful one. It demonstrates the wasted energy in groups where trust is lacking. In a "real" environment there are few games, freeing up attention to focus on the customer and the competition. It is a competitive weapon that is sustainable.

The Ex-CEO of SAS, Jan Carlson used the term "moments of truth" to describe all customer interfaces with employees of Scandinavian Airlines. Every time an employee interfaced with a customer, it was considered a golden opportunity to demonstrate company values. Without customers, there was no company. It put the customer out in front of the thinking process and allowed a constant reminder of the corporate vision.

As a leader, you have the same "moment of truth" whenever you interact with your associates. As you develop and use the techniques in the next sections, you will use each "moment of truth" as a golden opportunity to build trust and teach others how to do it. As a result, your leadership capability will increase dramatically.

The Transactional Nature of Trust

Trust is not a group phenomenon. It is individual. Leaders interact with many people and build trust-based relationships with each of them. Trust between people may be compared to a bank account, where actions consistent with shared values represent deposits and inconsistent actions represent withdrawals. The trust level of a group is the aggregate of the balances of individuals making up the group.

Every action, word, or decision between individuals either adds to, or detracts from, the balance. It is a very sensitive system that can be affected by subconscious thoughts or small gestures. Making small or medium deposits is easy, but large deposits are rare. Unfortunately, withdrawals can be large and devastating. The entire balance can be wiped out in a single action. As a leader, you need to prevent this by making all your actions consistent with what employees hear you say.

By understanding the transactional nature of trust, you can impact the account value in positive ways. Making continual deposits to the account over time builds trust efficiently so the balance can survive a withdrawal. Being conscious of the effect of withdrawals makes you less likely to make them. The challenge is to recognize how others interpret your words and actions.

Everyone has a frame of reference built from all personal experiences to date. You use this framework to judge everything, and because it is a distillation of your life experiences, you believe it without question.

A college classmate of mine illustrated this by wearing a button containing three of the most significant words in the English language, "I Am Right." He meant it as a joke, but there was wisdom behind the humor. We all walk around with an invisible button declaring, "I am right." If another person does not agree with that judgment, there is a

disconnection. Because "I am right," then you must be wrong!

In "Principle-Centered Leadership", Steven Covey concurs:

> "The root cause of almost all people problems is the basic communication problem – people do not listen with empathy. They listen from within their autobiography... Perception and credibility problems may ultimately result in complicated knots, what we often call 'personality conflicts' or 'communication breakdowns.' Credibility problems are far more difficult to resolve, primarily because each of the people involved thinks he sees the world as it is rather than as he is. Unaware of the distortion in his own perception, his attitude is this: 'If you disagree with me, in my eyes you are automatically wrong, simply because I am sure that I am right.' "

The phenomenon of judging from your own frame of reference goes on thousands of times every day. It is unavoidable and is the basis of most conflict. You have a great advantage if you can see this happening and intervene, but since you are a player in these transactions, not a neutral observer, it takes tremendous effort. That is why you must train yourself to recognize the moment and resist natural instincts. When you do, you become a stronger leader.

Trustbuilders and Trustbusters

Act in Ways Consistent with Values and Vision

The key to building trust starts with the framework described in Chapter 2. By establishing a shared vision along with values, behaviors and a strategic plan, you have created a pact with your team and a common frame of reference. As you conduct daily activities, there are hundreds of opportunities to act in a manner consistent with the pact. The challenge is to recognize when you are not doing this. Most people are unaware when they are inconsistent because they react according to their own automatic thinking process. They cannot see themselves as others do and are blind to any inconsistency.

For example, as a leader, I see my own consistency as 100% because "I am right." Everything I do or say is justified and consistent with the vision. If not, I would do something else.

The trouble arises when I add another person. In the eyes of that person, my consistency is far from 100%. With extreme care, I may be able to achieve 60-70% but inevitably I will appear inconsistent and create a disconnect. Now one of two things can occur.

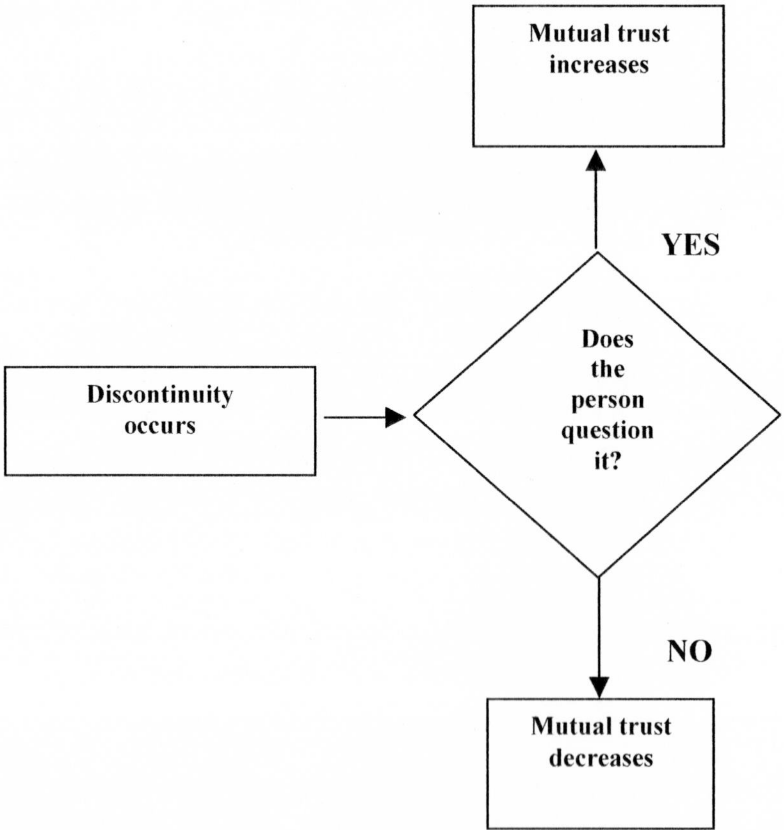

First, the other person can say or do nothing. They just don't want to talk about it. This reaction would normally seem the safer one. Why would someone remain silent in the face of a discontinuity (as most of the time they do)? It is out of insecurity and fear. There have been previous opportunities to voice a contrary opinion where this person felt punished rather than reinforced for voicing a dissenting opinion. It is just not safe to do it. We used to call such episodes "CTO's," short for career threatening opportunities. Unfortunately, they occur too frequently.

What happens to trust in this situation? It goes down! The person has less trust in me because I appear hypocritical, acting inconsistent with our values, behaviors, or vision. My trust in them *also goes down* because my subconscious knows something is wrong, but the other person remains silent. Remember, I firmly believe my actions were 100% consistent with our pact. Trust is reduced on both sides and, if this is a substantial issue, trust goes down dramatically.

Contrast that with a scenario where the other person verbalizes the problem immediately because it is safe to voice a contrary opinion. This is possible because an environment of trust has been built over a period of time. People know this kind of input is welcome.

Here the outlook is much brighter. We can have meaningful dialog on the discontinuity. I can reverse my action with a statement like "You're right, I didn't think of it that way. I'll reverse my decision. Thanks for pointing out my gaff." I could hold my ground with "I really appreciate your pointing out the inconsistency. I still believe my decision was right, but I'm glad you had the courage to speak up so I know there is a problem. If you are having trouble with it, others might too. Let me explain why I don't think it's wise to reverse the decision and see if you agree." Either way, the trust level goes up in the mind of each of us. I have been listening. I know the other person is leveling with me. The other person knows he has been heard and his opinion respected.

Invite Open Dialog when a Conflict is Perceived

Warren Bennis writes: "One of the best ways to build trust is by deep listening. It's the most powerful dynamic of human interaction when people feel they're being heard. Listening doesn't mean agreeing, but it does mean having the empathetic reach to understand another."

The best way to build trust through open dialog is to:

1. Encourage people to speak up if they think you are compromising the foundation developed in Chapter Two.
2. Reinforce them when they do it, no matter how it hurts at first. Listen actively and make them glad they brought it up.
3. Take the appropriate corrective action or help people think through the apparent paradox.

The first step is mechanical and pretty simple. At first there will be very few who point out issues. They are not convinced it is really safe. Keep asking and make sure you follow the second step every time. The third step emphasizes your sincerity and commitment to the vision.

Now you have an automatic correcting force, as described in Chapter Two. If something is out of line, people will tell you, enabling correction before much damage is done. Using this method you can establish an environment where honest feelings are shared and there are no large trust issues. The result is that people in your organization interface with you gladly, spend far less time fretting, and engage more energy pursuing the vision. There will be less gossip and fewer rumors. Over time, there will be less reluctance to challenge, and the best people outside your organization will ask if they can join your group. You will also see fewer Dilbert cartoons posted on the bulletin boards. The culture will have a sustainable competitive advantage. Success is easier.

This method works, but it needs constant tending. Persist. The more you practice, the easier it becomes. People get discouraged by external events and trust is fragile, so withdrawals will occur. The important thing is to keep the dialog open.

Sometimes, even with the best leaders, trust can be compromised for a time due to circumstances beyond their control. It is like an explosion, where hundreds of issues are being thrust at the leader all at once. In a state of overload, it is impossible to handle all issues perfectly.

Being a leader often means being unpopular for a time. Great leaders always seek to maximize trust, whatever the situation, and realize there will be rough times and setbacks along the way.

During these times, the number and severity of painful issues goes up dramatically. You will have an easier time maintaining trust if you are always open to new ideas or critiques.

Be Open to New Ideas

Every day, leaders hear a steady stream of ideas from many stakeholders. Each one has the seeds of greatness, but many require an open mind because they don't fit conventional thinking or seem tangential to the mission. Often these come up in a meeting environment or public interaction. Your reaction to ideas sets the climate for their evaluation.

Avoid prejudging the intent of people making suggestions. It is better to err on the side of being gracious, allowing nearly all ideas to be considered valid, than to cut off someone who had noble intent but difficulty expressing himself publicly.

If an idea seems "off the wall" say, "That's interesting. I would never have thought of it. On the surface it doesn't seem to fit, but let's look at it more carefully. You may be onto something here." Get your team to identify things they like about the idea, along with the challenges it represents. If you do this honestly, you will uncover creative approaches that will move the organization forward. In addition, the person presenting the idea will realize that all suggestions, no matter how unusual, have value as long as they are sincere.

The cardinal rule is, never let someone feel belittled or embarrassed for bringing an idea to the table unless they are obviously trying to sabotage the discussion. Look for the merit in every suggestion instead of the fatal flaw. It may not be valid in its present form, but suitably modified it could be quite valuable.

In some cases you will encounter a disruptive "grandstander" who continually interrupts and won't let you or others have the floor. Once it is obvious this person is out to derail the agenda, he must be silenced. The best approach is to say, "I appreciate these suggestions, but, in all fairness, we need to allow others a chance to be heard."

Don't Put People Off

People advance ideas because they believe their opinions have value. Putting people off is a common mistake. Someone has a concern and tries to point it out. You are focusing all your energy on another issue and brush off the distraction. Doing that too often sends an unspoken message that you don't want to hear about inconsistencies or concerns. That undermines trust.

Putting people off temporarily is often necessary to keep conversations focused on urgent matters. If you get back to them quickly, it provides a trust-building opportunity. People know you are busy and the follow-up demonstrates that you care about them. Their issue may seem inconsequential compared to other things facing you at the moment, but it is important to them. A few hours later, people have often forgotten their issue. It now seems inconsequential compared to other things. When you remind them of it, they are amazed and beam with pride. You have made a major trust deposit.

A typical trustbuilding exchange might sound like this:

> Boss: "In the meeting this morning, you voiced a concern about the training budget. We couldn't get into it then, but I made a note to get back to you. I checked the figures with the HR department. What was your concern?"
>
> Employee: "It isn't a big deal. I just wanted to be sure we weren't going to get cut in the training area. It always seems to be the place they cut first."
>
> Boss: "Well, it looks like we did get a 20% cut, so your concern was valid. We'll need help deciding which programs have the most impact. I will make sure upper management knows how passionate you are about maintaining training dollars if possible."

Employee: "Thanks for the good word. I get upset when they cut training, but they must have difficult tradeoffs when money is tight. I hope we can prevent further cuts."

Boss: "I'm glad you can see both sides. I would love to have you on the committee to decide which programs to cut. You have a great perspective and your energy keeps everyone engaged. Can you spare the time?"

Employee: "Sure, I'll do what I can."

Another technique is to ask the employee to send a brief e-mail with the concern or question. Composing the note helps to clarify the issue and take out some of the emotion. Plus, have a tangible reminder as a cue.

Following up takes only a moment, but the goodwill it creates lasts for weeks. In his book "Iacocca", Lee Iacocca put it this way: "You don't have to accept every single suggestion, but if you don't get back to the guy and say, 'Hey that idea was terrific,' and pat him on the back, he'll never give you another one. That kind of communication lets people know they really count." Always make people glad they voiced their idea or concern.

Reinforce People who Challenge

Punishing people when they bring up inconsistencies creates a trust withdrawal. This is particularly damaging because it diminishes the potential for future trust-building dialog. Stephen Covey describes it this way in his book, "Principle-Centered Leadership": "Too often we punish honest, open expressions or questions. We upbraid, judge, belittle, embarrass. Others learn to cover up, to protect themselves, to not ask. The greatest single barrier to rich, honest communication is the tendency to criticize and judge."

Reinforcing people who point out problems builds trust. Once it starts, you have more opportunities for additional growth of trust. If an associate points out an inconsistency, this is a teachable moment where you have an opportunity to demonstrate the art of building trust.

This is one of the most difficult things in business. It is only natural to become defensive when someone is poking at your actions. You need a mechanism to allow reinforcement of open dialog on difficult subjects.

Try to develop a reflex reaction to hearing things that are upsetting. When a person tells you something hard to swallow (especially if it's about you), human nature causes you to go into "fight or flight" thinking. Instead, train yourself to resist the temptation to lash back when someone points out a problem. They are giving you a golden opportunity to build trust, and besides, their analysis is often right! Internalize the point and let it sink in while remaining calm. As you "count to 10", identify how you can respond in a way that makes the person glad they brought it up. This is an extremely difficult skill to develop but the extent you do it will determine your expertise as a true leader.

Noel Tichy described how employees speak out in no uncertain terms only when a leader has created an open and honest shop. More often, people simply become demoralized and ignore the values if the leader does, so getting "nailed to the wall" by people on occasion is a sign of things actually going right in the organization. It shows there is some level of trust.

Not getting enough pushback is a telltale sign that trust is compromised. It is a very sensitive barometer of trust. When things get quiet, do not assume everything is okay. Usually it's the opposite. Find out what is wrong and deal with it immediately. The analogy in nature is how the crickets stop chirping when danger is near.

As you reinforce people for being open, do it in ways that enhance individual self-esteem. When people speak out, they are going out on a limb emotionally. Reinforce them for taking that risk. Good leaders imagine themselves on the receiving end of these exchanges and try to follow the golden rule. If you are wrong, don't be too proud or let your ego block you from a humble apology.

Publicly Admit Mistakes

All leaders make mistakes. When you encourage others to point them out, it's a good lesson in humility. It puts your ego on the back burner where it belongs. A central theme of this book is building trust by encouraging others to point out mistakes.

When you reinforce and respond well to input:

1. You increase trust with the person sharing the input.
2. You build trust more widely through a public response.

When a leader makes a mistake and recognizes it, the common reaction is to finesse the situation. Significant energy is spent trying to hide the gaff or blame some outside situation for it. Rather than face the ugly truth, human nature tries to mitigate the damage by pretending it didn't happen or explaining it away. Even worse, some people try to shift responsibility to others.

It is like the politician caught in an extramarital affair. First, he denies it. Then, when confronted with evidence, he downplays it. Finally, he tries to shift focus to another important topic. The paradox is that this flailing around does significantly more damage than a confession and apology at the outset.

The same holds true for every leader when a mistake occurs. It is better to assemble the people immediately and give a "mea culpa" speech than to spend a lot of energy trying to duck the issue. In fact, it actually ***enhances*** your reputation as you demonstrate honesty and humility. It also helps the reputation of the person bringing up the issue. They feel better knowing their input made a difference.

People understand and will forgive making wrong steps in the pressure cooker. They won't forgive the "weasel" that goes around trying to make himself look good whatever the situation. Don't shy away from the opportunities to display vulnerability. They are really more opportunities than threats.

Scott Adams, creator of the Dilbert series, has made a killing on the gaffs of clueless, pointy-haired bosses. Don't get caught in that scenario. Publicly admitting a mistake and looking for a better way will eliminate dozens of Dilbert-like discussions in the break rooms across your area.

Do a through postmortem when mistakes occur. This analysis step is often neglected in the rush of new issues. Spending time understanding the situation can prevent other problems in the future. It also demonstrates the value of dissecting failures to determine root cause. You and your team can learn a great deal by studying failures and asking what you could have done to prevent them. Take the insights and generalize them to cover other situations. The effectiveness of the whole team will improve. As a leader, you should cherish this insight because it reduces trial and error. Some leaders make the same mistakes many times before learning how to avoid them.

Follow up on all Commitments

In today's environment, most leaders are over-committed, which can lead to mistakes and omissions. Following up on commitments is essential, but often neglected by busy leaders. It is so easy to say to someone, "I'll get back to you on this," and then forget it in the crunch of critical work. You may rationalize and say, "Well, it wasn't really a promise and they know how busy I am. This is only a minor issue anyway." That kind of thinking will harpoon your trust-building efforts. If building trust is all about consistency, nothing is more basic than doing what you say.

Whenever you make a commitment, no matter how small, make sure you do it.

Tips on Commitment:

- When you promise something, put a time frame on it. Rather than "I'll get back to you," say "I'll get back to you on this by the end of tomorrow. If I get derailed and you don't hear from me by then, please give me a call." The person knows you really do intend to answer their question.
- Keep an action item list. Whatever form, whether a 3"x5" card in your pocket or a handheld computer, get the item written down along with a time frame to answer. It helps to

write it in front of the person with the concern. You can say, "Just a second - let me jot that down so I don't forget to get back to you." The person feels honored that you are considering the issue strongly enough to document it and will tell everyone about the exchange during the next break.

- If you delegate the issue to another person for follow-up, make sure they preface their response with, "Bob asked me to get back to you on this question." Also, make sure your agent confirms with you when it is done. Cross it off your list when your agent tells you it is closed, not when you delegate it to him. In some cases, you should circle back to the person with a note or call saying, "I asked Mike to get back to you on your concern about the slippery floors. Did you hear from him and was his response satisfactory?" Doing that gives you the opportunity to jack up any agents that shirk their duty. In a staff meeting you can say something like, "I have been following up when I ask some of you to get back to employees on their concerns. Some of them have complained that their concern is downplayed. When I ask you to act as my agent, I expect you will keep working on it until the situation is resolved satisfactorily to the employee. If you can't resolve their concern, get back to me. Don't let it drop."

- Use handwritten notes to people. A brief note, along with a "thank you for bringing this up," will be prized by the individual and shared in the break room. Be careful to use a tangible note only when the response is positive and difficult to misinterpret. Otherwise, you may find your note tacked to the break room bulletin board next to a Dilbert cartoon. For difficult issues, it is always better to deal face-to-face.

Closure on action items is not confined to personal discussions. The same logic holds when you promise something to a group. If you say, "I will make a decision on overtime by noon," make sure they hear from you on that schedule. It is important to state a deadline or things tend to stretch out. You may think a week to unveil a new organization is reasonable, but for some people it feels like, "he promised to do something about that but never got back to us."

Show a High Level of Trust

Trust has to work both ways. People need to trust you and you need to trust them. If you really trust people, it shows. There are hundreds of ways you demonstrate faith in people to do the right thing. This is something you cannot fake. Be willing to experience the negative consequences of a mistake made by someone you trust. That is a hard lesson but, if you can do it, the rewards far outweigh the penalties.

Occasionally you will have to eat crow because someone was late with a submission, but most of the time people will be giving extra effort because you have faith in them. When people describe why they go the extra mile for an outstanding leader, they often say, "She believes in me. I would do anything to keep from disappointing her." When you put your faith in people, 95% of the time they will go way beyond normal effort and 5% of the time they will drop the ball. Those are very good odds.

You will be amazed at the creativity and initiative people exhibit when you trust them. Self-esteem will be high, and they will enjoy the work even while pushing themselves to the limit. Occasionally, they may over-commit and fall short of expectations. Handle this with empathy and it will be a learning opportunity, a chance to enhance the relationship rather than a time of remorse. Nobody feels good when they fail. As a leader, you have the opportunity to help people through that letdown with grace and class.

Allow People to Fail

We grow more by trying and failing than by taking the safe course. Leaders who protect people from failure are holding the reigns too tightly. People need to pursue their own path sometimes, even if it's not one you would have chosen. It is a delicate balance. You don't want people to fail, but they must be free to innovate. Let people do their job and don't "micromanage." Usually things will work out for the best. You will also be getting the maximum energy available. People work twice as hard to make their own ideas work.

If people run into problems, become a coach and help them learn from the experience. This is a good opportunity to reinforce their initiative. You do need to be forthright that an error occurred. Don't sugarcoat the situation, but manage the discussion to maintain self-esteem.

When people try but fail, the best advice is to follow the Golden Rule. Simple kindness is often overlooked in the rush of critical work. If you reverse roles and treat the employee the way you would want to be treated, little damage will be done. In addition, you can help adjust their workload or working conditions to enhance their chances for success in the future.

Tell the Truth

Never try to snow people, individually or in groups. When leaders watch their words so they are not technically lying, but also not telling the truth, people know it instinctively. Recall when former President Bill Clinton answered a question with "That depends on what the meaning of the word, 'is', is." Everyone in the country saw through that smokescreen and his reputation was damaged even more.

Here is another example. Let's suppose there is a rumor going around that your plant will be closing soon. You have a meeting and someone asks you point-blank if the plant will close. Rather than say "I don't know about any final decision", try: "I am privy to discussions that could affect us, but I cannot share them yet because they are confidential. I do know they have not made a decision yet. I can tell you we expect a decision by next Tuesday, and you can count on a report from me on or before that time." With either statement, people will be on edge (you really can't prevent that), but with the second one you have accomplished 3 things. First, you are telling them the truth and they know it. Second, you are giving them the best information you can, along with a time frame for further information. Third, you are assuring them that they will hear from you personally as soon as you can reveal a decision.

Dealing with the issue of truth is a study in itself. There are numerous perspectives, from being consistent with your values to not hiding facts from people. The key point for this book is to realize ***your integrity with people is directly coupled to the trust level you achieve***. Leaders who place the highest value on truth will attain and sustain higher levels of trust than leaders who attempt to finesse things. Realize that people are more perceptive at picking up lies or half-truths than you think. As you seek to model integrity in your own arena, it models the way for others. Another way to emphasize integrity is to reinforce people when you observe them making the hard choice to do the right thing despite the consequences.

Reinforce Honest Ethical Behaviors

Acting with integrity often takes courage. Sometimes people reveal things because of their ethics that cause them considerable discomfort. I recall one worker in a high tech production area who let us know of sabotage being done by another worker. He had been threatened with harm to himself and his family if he tattled, but if he didn't, the customer would get defective product. He brought the information forth because of his integrity and connection with the business, even though he could get stabbed for doing it. We immediately fired the saboteur and promoted the whistle-blower. We also arranged for security for him and his family until the danger had subsided.

That is an extreme case, but people often go outside their comfort zone because of ethics. Make sure you reward them personally and make a big deal of it to others. Honest behavior needs to be reinforced as much as possible. It is another moment of truth and an opportunity to let people know your convictions.

Eradicate Substance Abuse

Unfortunately, substance abuse in the workplace is common. In production areas, there are often drug rings that sell illegal substances. People can become part of the sub-culture before they are even aware of it. You can find situations where people are petrified of the drug dealer in their midst. They want to get rid of the person, but don't know how to do it safely.

As a leader, you need to be alert to the signs of strain and get things under control. Once you are aware, if you turn your back and let the problem fester, people will lose faith in you. It may take a major intervention to get rid of the cancer. Work with the Corporate Security people, along with HR, Medical, and local law enforcement agencies to formulate an action plan. People will look to you for help and trust you will provide it.

Release Information Wisely

Everyone in your organization needs to have information about the business and their part in it. Withholding information can destroy trust. The business case for keeping certain material confidential often doesn't hold water. When you feel obligated to hold some information private, challenge the assumptions. Don't tacitly accept a gag order if it doesn't make sense to you. Check with the people advocating it and debate the wisdom of disclosure versus withholding information.

These negotiations are usually with higher levels of management, the legal community, or Human Relations. You may not have a choice about withholding information and need to follow orders without question. If you can't release information, ask what you can say to reduce the gossip and rumors.

Discourage Gossip and Rumors

Rumors in the workplace deflect energy from pursuit of the vision. When the leader engages in gossip or rumors, it is particularly debilitating. I once knew a department manager who would come into my office and say, "Don't tell anybody else, but I heard on the Q.T. that . . . " Then, later, I would hear him telling the same thing to another person. People had little respect for the integrity of this person; he had loose lips.

As a leader, you set the tone. By engaging in gossip, you tacitly give others permission to do the same. Also, if you leak information to certain people, you are playing favorites in a very destructive way. Stick to the facts and keep busy with your vision.

If someone tries to engage you in idle gossip, say something like "I don't try to guess these things until an announcement is made. I used to, but found that I usually guessed wrong. I was just wasting valuable time when I could have been pursuing our vision."

Never Talk Behind People's Backs

Similar to gossip, but more hurtful, is talking about a problem employee with another worker. You send a signal that you can't be trusted. The other person is forced to conclude, "If he is telling me this about Barbara, I wonder what he tells other people about me?" It does not pay to have loose lips regarding people issues. It demonstrates a lack of integrity and trust will definitely suffer.

The logic is the same even if the message has a more helpful tone. If you tell someone on the assembly line, "I hope Roger can get better control of his break time so there is less stress on the rest of you," you are on very thin ice. If there is a problem with Roger's use of break time, address it with him, not anyone else. Communicate with people directly, not through others. If you try to "relay" information to someone through another person, chances are the message will be distorted and you will appear manipulative.

A leader who builds trust treats everyone fairly. By talking behind someone's back, you are unfair to both the person you talk about and the person you talk to. It will impact group dynamics in an unhealthy way.

Don't Play Favorites

Being fair can sometimes be difficult. All leaders play favorites to some extent, whether they want to or not. Part of leadership is to put the best people in position to be successful. This is a delicate area with potentially large impact. In the daily pressure cooker, if you assign work trying to please everyone, group performance will suffer. No matter what the choice, some people perceive these actions as "playing favorites," so trust and credibility can be compromised. How can you deal with this dichotomy?

Placement of people should be an open process and part of expected behavior. Openly discuss and agree upon a policy to select individuals for assignments. It should not be left to chance or the knee-jerk judgment of the leader without some level of influence by those affected.

For example, in some areas there may be an "open posting" process, where people volunteer to be considered for assignments. There is a screening and evaluation process, often including peer evaluation, before a selection and announcement. In this case, the leader could have final decision rights, but with strong input from an evaluation team. Whatever the rules, they should be well understood and adhered to unless an emergency prevents it.

Unions often have a set procedure for selecting people. These rules must be well documented, internalized, and followed. Union situations create many challenges to establishing trust within a group. It is difficult enough to balance things when there are two sides negotiating. Unions bring a third element to the equation that increases complexity. It is not the purpose of this book to describe union issues and challenges. If your situation includes a union, be aware that all of the issues described here become much more complex.

Selection of people for certain assignments is an art. In many situations, such as shop floor assignments, decisions are made many times a day. Be sensitive to the issue of favorites and take some risk by stepping outside the normal pattern. It doesn't take many shocking calls for a leader to beat the stigma of always calling on a few favorites. It also keeps the so-called "favorites" on their toes to realize they are not always the heir apparent, while allowing you to test people in stretch roles for growth.

When communicating a decision, if a personnel selection is your "usual" choice, preempt grumbling about playing favorites by a statement addressing it upfront. Try something like, "I selected George to head our new waste team. He is the best qualified for this critical assignment because his background in 'XYZ' is exactly what the situation requires. I want to be fair to everyone, so if any of you have concerns about this please let me know." This kind of approach normally tones down the angst, as people are aware of your sensitivity. Use this technique sparingly, and don't talk down to people. This is a situation where you may think you are being sensitive, but come across as manipulative or clueless. If there is a real issue, people have been given an open invitation for dialog. In an environment of trust, concerned people will respond. Be sure to make them glad they did.

Hallmarks of Trust

Have you ever been in a situation where you had to choose words carefully, like you were walking on eggs? This is indicative of a low trust situation where communication is tedious at best. In this hostile environment people are ready to pounce on any opportunity to misinterpret or bend whatever is being presented. You must be hypersensitive to every word and inflection to avoid people misreading your intent. Covey describes it this way:

> "When the relationship is unified and harmonious, we can almost communicate without words. Where there is high trust and good feelings we don't have to 'watch our words' at all. We can smile or not and still communicate meaning and achieve understanding. When the relationship is not well established, a chapter of words won't be sufficient to communicate meaning because meanings are not found in words – they are found in people."

Once you achieve an environment of trust, all forms of communication become easier. Big mistakes are rare because any small communication glitch will be surfaced and dealt with before it becomes an issue. You can relax and be yourself in all your communications.

In areas where trust is high, you can see lots of evidence of it. I always describe it as a backyard in winter. When there are rabbits in the neighborhood, there is ample evidence all over the lawns. Maybe the analogy is a bit gross, but it works for me. Groups who have high trust act and react differently from those with lower trust levels. There is an esprit de corps among people. They laugh more and seem to have a great time being together. They struggle with problems just like everyone else, but they climb over them quickly and move on.

The body language in these groups is one of love and support for one another. People will not tolerate backbiting or badmouthing. Respect is on their faces. They volunteer to help each other willingly and go out of their way to be kind. When they describe their improvement programs, they beam with pride. If you walk into a conference room full of people with high trust, it takes only a few seconds to sense it. People don't even have to talk. Unfortunately, even in the best groups, things are not amicable all the time. Occasionally, there will be setbacks and problems to overcome.

A hallmark of a trusting environment is that letdowns don't impact the climate very long. Human beings are fallible. No two people can work in close proximity without one letting the other down eventually. If an atmosphere of trust has been nurtured, the event will trigger an exchange that is open and honest. "When you were late, I felt bad because it meant I would need to cover for both of us." This is then followed by reinforcement for pointing out the gaff: "I really appreciate that you told me. I didn't realize the impact it was having on you. I'll try to be on time from now on." The bad feelings never get a chance to escalate. In fact, the existence of a gaff only ends up ***enhancing*** the relationship because it is extinguished so quickly.

In an atmosphere of trust, you get tremendous progress from improvement initiatives because disconnects will quickly surface. This avoids pursuing a mechanical improvement program that lacks support from all constituents.

The suggestions offered in this chapter will work, provided there is good consensus among the team. Test for this commitment often and don't operate in a vacuum.

You can benefit from these ideas as an individual contributor, but you cannot effectively drive them in the organization above you. You need the support of your boss and peers. Frequently, that is a major stumbling block. What you can do is embrace and use these tools *in the environment you control.* Demonstrate their power by example and offer to expand the ideas beyond your current boundaries. If you get pushback, don't pressure people. Instead just continue to gain the mileage in your area and lead by example.

Chapter 5 - Level of Communication

Effective communication is critical for building trust. This chapter is about communicating without ambiguity. I address this from the point of view of the leader, but the concepts are applicable to all people in the organization.

The objective of all communication is to accurately transfer information from one person to others. A leader must internalize incoming information in all forms and craft outgoing information in ways that translate concepts. Let's look at incoming information first.

Skill areas that are important for every leader:

- Being accessible – how easy is it for people to get their message through to the leader?
- Interpreting body language – being sensitive to the subtle human signals that contain the majority of information in any interaction. These must be internalized, decoded, and analyzed in the context of each interface to achieve correct exchange of information.
- Listening well – the ability to understand and decode information accurately with a recognition that incoming data is subject to the listener's internal biases. Suspending judgment, rebuttal or preparation of response until all the data has been received.
- Facing Reality – listening well, even when the input is upsetting or challenging.
- Reading between the lines – gaining information from things left unsaid.

- Testing for understanding – not being satisfied with simply hearing and interpreting incoming signals, but understanding the perspective and intent of the sender. What are the political implications at work in this information exchange?
- Getting the right data – assembling and sorting all forms of data that put information in the correct context, making the data complete.
- Interpreting validity of data – testing to identify if the input represents the view of a single outlier or if it is part of a pattern shared by many. Often incoming data is biased by the sender and may only partially reflect reality.
- Recognizing the implications – does this new information require action or is it simply useful as additional background data?

There is a lot going on when a leader is on the receiving end of communication. It requires a great deal of concentration and discipline to receive and decode information accurately. An even more daunting task occurs on the sending side.

Skills required for good outward communication:

- Defining your audience – will this communication be personal, small group, or mass communication? Will this message be crafted for people at the same level, up the organization chain or downward?
- Using the right mode of communication – is it delivered verbally, in writing, graphically, experientially, or through others?
- Relaying context – has the leader communicated how this message fits into the mosaic of other previous data? Does this new information make other data obsolete? If so, has that been clarified?
- Showing congruity – how well is the message aligned with stated values, vision, behaviors, and plans.

- Being user friendly – is the message easy to understand, internalize, and remember?
- Being unambiguous – does the message leave little room for misinterpretation? Is it crystal clear and uncluttered by excessive confusing rhetoric?
- Verifying transfer of the real message – has the leader tested to insure the information has been accurately conveyed? Do people understand both the technical data and the intent?

A lot of mental gymnastics goes on in the brain of a leader, which impacts the quality of communications. Applying these skills successfully in the context of everyday interactions is a major task that governs the trust level of the leader. Here are some ideas you can use to improve your effectiveness.

Communicating with individuals and small informal groups

First, be accessible. Regardless of how busy you are, find time to interact with people when needed. People need to know there is an open channel. Be gracious with your time since it really is all you have. Show up in their workplace from time to time, just to chat. You will find people appreciate it, and you will be setting an example of good leadership.

In these interfaces, it is essential to show a genuine interest in what the people are thinking. Draw people out enough to hear their problems and let them know you are grateful for the input. Smalltalk is okay to get the ball rolling, but you are mostly there to find out issues and understand people better.

You enhance trust between yourself and other people when you show genuine interest in their point of view. This requires more listening and less talking. To practice this, assess the quality of your communication immediately after you interface with someone. Strive to have your listening time be at least twice your talking time.

Practice "management by walking around."

Keep yourself plugged into what people are saying. If a manager's visit to the shop floor is a special event, honest communication will suffer. Show enough presence so it is not a special event when you are around. A litmus test for this is to watch the body language of workers as you approach them in the workplace. If they maintain constant body language, they are comfortable with you. If they stiffen up, there is a barrier to open communication.

If you are a high-test leader, you have little time for breaks. You probably work straight through lunch and never slow down for about 12 hours per day. Even with that intensity, try to find a few minutes several times a week to go to a break room and sit with whoever is there. Ask, "Mind if I join you?" and "What's happening?" Then shut up and listen. If you do this often enough, people won't see it as unusual, like you are checking up on the length of their breaks, etc. It is amazing how much information you can pick up in that forum that is unavailable any other way.

If you don't have time for this, it's a problem of priority. Mark your calendar and tell your administrative person this "people time" is not to be bumped. Working with people is more enjoyable than most meetings anyway. Sending a substitute to a management meeting so you can improve understanding of your people gives a strong positive signal of your priorities. However, be careful not to over use this technique and end up in trouble with management. Balance your time carefully, but be sure to interface with people regularly. Prepare yourself to internalize the whole message, not just the words. Become a master of reading body language.

Study Body Language

Understanding body language is essential to good communications. In his book, "People Skills," Dr. Robert Bolton stresses the importance of body language:

> "A person cannot not communicate. Though she may decide to stop talking, it is impossible for her

> to stop behaving. The behavior of a person – her facial expressions, posture, gestures, and other actions – provide an uninterrupted stream of information and a constant source of clues to the feelings she is experiencing. The reading of body language, therefore, is one of the most significant skills of good listening."

People constantly scream out their reactions with gestures. Learning to read these clues is an art form you must master. Formal study is an easy way to enhance your skill. A helpful book is "How to Read a Person Like a Book," by Nierenberg and Calero. There is also an assessment tool to test proficiency, called "Silence Speaks Louder Than Words," published by Organization Design and Development, Inc.

While on assignment in Mexico, I learned the power of nonverbal information. Not knowing enough Spanish to follow the business arguments in heated meetings, I just observed body language, including voice inflections. Incredibly, when someone stopped to brief me in English on the last 45 minutes, there was no need. I knew exactly what they were talking about, who proposed what, and their rationale. Much to their amazement, I described the politics at the root of the disagreement accurately without understanding a word.

Words can even hinder understanding because they distract conscious attention *away* from what is going on in the hearts of people. Dialog creates the necessity to focus on words, internalize them, and figure out an appropriate response. While most of us are "listening" to others, we are usually preparing to talk. That reduces focus on the majority of the message which is nonverbal. Balance attention among all forms of input and continually hone your skill at picking up nonverbal cues.

My mentor had an uncanny ability to read people. It seemed there was no way of fooling him. He always had your true feelings digested before you had gotten past the hors d'oeuvres. I once asked him how he could tell if someone was putting him on. He said, "I just watch to see if the words match the body language. If they do, I know I am hearing truth. If not, I know there is another agenda going on." He had learned the art of balancing conscious attention between verbal and nonverbal cues. It had become second nature, giving him a significant advantage.

Reading body language is a critical part of the technique called "reflective" (sometimes called "active") listening.

Reflective Listening

Most leaders could improve their listening skills. Few are experts at reflective listening, which is the most positive method of ensuring tight communications. With this technique, you pay close attention to body language around what is being said, internalize it, then, at an appropriate time, feed back your understanding by paraphrasing the point. Establish a daily routine of practicing reflective listening and you will enhance your leadership.

Ironically, we tend to avoid reflective listening in situations where it could be of highest value. Listening skills are most needed in highly emotional discussions, when people bring up a major problem. Most leaders get embroiled in the discussion and focus on fixing the issue, rather than truly hearing what the other person is saying. Often the frustrated employee leaves the office unfulfilled because the domineering boss resolved the wrong problem. "She spent all our time together helping me reword the proposal and never heard my main point, that we need more time to get the right data before the proposal will be valid." Everyone can relate to that kind of problem.

Reflective listening must be done well to be effective. If the reflections are clumsy, poorly timed, or overly done, they can confuse or annoy the other person. The best antidote is to watch the body language of the other person carefully.

Good listening skills are also important when communicating with groups. Learn to take cues from your audience both as a group and as individuals.

Communicating to Large Groups

Marginal communicators put their audiences to sleep. You see people with glazed eyes trying to be polite and hoping the agony will be over soon. How do you avoid this? In communicating with large groups, foster a special quality of "connectedness." Hold the audience in your hand. Make sure they hear and *internalize* what is being said.

First, consider whether the facilities and your audience are in proper condition for communication. In "The Pursuit of Wow", Tom Peters said, "You may think you are the world's greatest speaker with a message of utmost urgency, but if the auditorium's air conditioning is on the fritz and the sound system is singing static – well, forget it."

Pay attention to the physical layout. Things like the aspect ratio of the room, the comfort of the chairs, the layout of tables, lighting, whether or not amplification is needed, all make a big difference in getting people to pay attention.

Temperature is another key variable, especially for long meetings. It is common for some to feel warm, while others are chilled. Test frequently if people are comfortable with the temperature, and do what you can to strike a good balance.

Some speakers ramble on, paying little attention to signals from the audience. They might go on for 2 ½ hours expecting the audience to grasp everything being said. After a couple cups of coffee, the average human being needs a break after 50-60 minutes. It is impossible to concentrate on a presentation when you urgently need to relieve yourself. Ignoring biological needs is inconsiderate and self-defeating. I guarantee, after 90 minutes most people have checked out. The only thing they want to hear is, "Let's take a 15 minute break." Do not promise your audience a break "in a couple minutes" then keep talking for 10 minutes. After 2-3 minutes, nobody will be listening to a word you are saying.

Read your audience like a book. Alter cadence and tone to keep listeners engaged. Make constant eye contact by scanning the group. If you see one person emotionally checked out, work on that person – maybe ask them a question - but get them engaged somehow. Use visual aids to enhance the presentation, so people can grasp complex issues with ease. These aids should be simple but compelling to the message. There must be no ambiguity.

Good speakers frequently test to determine if people are getting the message. This is like the famous TV chef, Emeril Lagasse, who turns to the audience several times a show with "are you with me so far?" This keeps people engaged in the presentation as if it were a personal discussion. Thinking of a speech as dialog is a helpful concept. The audience gives you verbal cues and body language. If you are skilled at reading them, you will insure people are with you throughout the presentation. In the end, they will have internalized your message. They may not like it or agree with it, but they definitely get the message. Reading audience body language also helps you know when they need a stretch break or if the temperature is too low.

I like to use silence as a means of getting audience attention. During a presentation, people are expecting a constant drone of words. As long as you are babbling up front, they can check out mentally and think about their upcoming fishing trip. When you stop talking, the anxiety level goes up with every second. "Why isn't he saying anything? What is happening here?" It is an extremely powerful tool. If you are the speaker and simply stop talking for 15-20 seconds, you will have everyone's full attention when you begin again. Do not overuse this tool. Once or twice in a 60 minute presentation is the maximum. More than that will alienate the audience.

Most speakers attempt to talk louder and faster when the audience is checking out mentally. The idea is to grab their attention by being more intrusive. Actually, the reverse is more effective. Speak very softly and slowly for a sentence or two to bring your audience back to consciousness.

Ask your audience questions to maintain the feel of dialog. Try alternating between rhetorical and literal questions to keep the audience involved. I like to walk into the audience space when asking questions. The physical presence of a speaker standing 5 feet away, rather than up front, makes people feel the questions are directed at them. An alternative to wandering into the audience is simply to look intently at one section of the room when you ask your question.

Good communication does not occur at the "head" level. Sure, we use the mouth to speak, the ears to hear, the brain to interpret, the eyes to see, etc. Real communication is deep in the gut. When you have internalized the message fully, it goes well into the body. Don't make the mistake of thinking you have communicated with someone because you have talked and they appear to have heard it. Verify what was taken in at the gut level.

With verbal communication you can verify the message was received more easily than with written communications.

Written & Electronic Communication that Works

Communicating in writing outside of e-mail is nearly a lost art. Great leaders take the time to write notes to individuals for reinforcement, knowing the recipient will read them many times over and be reinforced each time. Something written is forever. Be careful what you write, but do use the technique often because it has special significance. People often keep a written reinforcement in their desk drawer for years or take it home to share with their family. Some notes even get framed or copied in a book, like Jack Welch's handwritten notes to his successor, Jeffrey Immelt.

When communicating electronically, it is easy to forget the messages are ***permanent and uncontrolled.*** With notes flying back and forth constantly, it feels like these "conversations" are private. They are not. An emotional e-mail forwarded to another person becomes a boomerang that may be shared with those who would take it incorrectly. Never send something on an unsecured electronic channel that you would not want shared broadly.

You rarely know about the damage directly since it is out of your line of sight. Typically, you will sense a change in body language with a cohort: a coolness that wasn't there before. You wonder what triggered it. Often it is the result of an e-mail you sent to a third party that got forwarded to this person, who was upset by your words.

Electronic phone messages are even more dangerous, because they contain voice inflection as well as words. Make sure you have a secure channel for personal messages to avoid having people forward embarrassing information.

A cardinal rule is, never send a note, letter, e-mail, or voice mail when you are angry. Your emotions will show through even if you try to avoid it, and you will regret your words. When someone sends you something that makes your blood boil, it's hard to remain mum until the rage is under control. Remembering this rule was a challenge for me. Many times the only way I survived was to write a blistering reply that vented my true feelings but not send it.

(Incidentally, it is best to store sensitive messages like this in a separate file saved to a floppy disk, rather than the corporate system.) In a few days, after the rage subsided, I would review the notes. I never sent any of those messages without major changes.

Coach your leaders to avoid a string of "e-mail grenades." If someone takes a cheap shot, just respond with a polite reply like "I received your e-mail and, while I have trouble agreeing with some of your points, I appreciate your candor." That gets the message across about issues but does so in a classy way. When you are tempted to strike back, just remember the adage, "Keep your words soft and sweet because you may have to eat them." Those who practice e-mail one-upmanship often appear foolish even when they are right.

Voice and e-mail systems can be helpful aids in leadership. They allow you to strategize with other leaders whenever a helpful thought arrives. I would often pull my lawn mower up to the house and jump off to send a message that popped into my mind on the back lawn. Without this convenience, many good ideas would not get captured. The ability to operate 24 hours a day without being a slave to the communication channels is a huge advantage.

A great deal of stress is created by differing habits with electronic messages. If you are a person who checks voice mail every three days, you will be annoyed with someone who sends out several messages a day. Likewise, you are bugging them because they expect a fast response and you don't give it.

Understand the expectations of others relative to electronic messages. For example, I tried to answer all voice messages within 4 hours (except during sleep time) and all e-mails within a day. Knowing this, my managers could meter their communications to match that style. They also knew that not answering me for several days would draw a complaint.

Failing to answer at all is an impolite habit. Sometimes it seems like there is a "black hole" where messages go in but answers never come out.

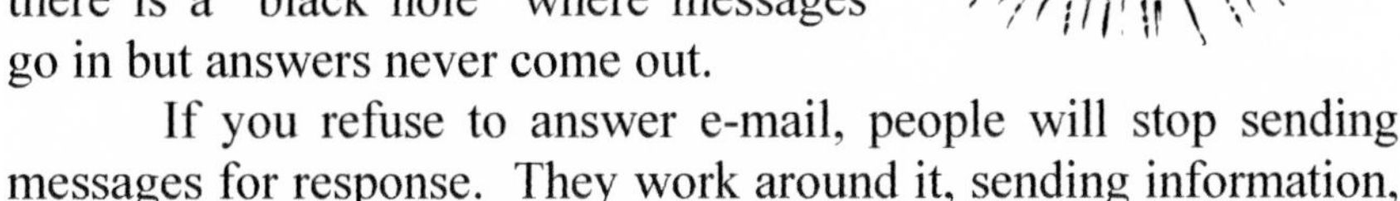

If you refuse to answer e-mail, people will stop sending messages for response. They work around it, sending information, but nothing serious. If your message service has receipts, you can see if the other party has opened your note, but don't assume any communication occurred unless you get meaningful feedback..

Resolve Communication Gaps

Communication gaps are more challenging for people who work in different locations. As a leader, you need to sense when to get polarized people together so adversarial attitudes won't undermine progress.

Video conferencing is helpful, but not a substitute for face to face communications. Issues tend to get resolved in the background or peripheral discussions and group body language is often misinterpreted in video conferencing.

Once I took on a project with a tight timeframe. It was a peripheral disk drive that had been languishing in development for 3 years. I was asked to lead the project on September 15th with a goal to have it on the market by year-end. It seemed impossible. The product did not work, and there would be at least 6 weeks of reliability testing after the bugs were worked out. A particular challenge was geographical. The drives were made in New York, the heads in Taiwan, and the media in San Diego. All had to work together for the system to be reliable.

Breaking down the failure modes, we discovered the heads needed redesign. Normally that would take 4-6 months, but we had only two weeks. I sent a group of engineers to Taiwan to work in the manufacturing facility. They had prototype parts in 6 days, with a steady supply forthcoming the next week. No amount of phone calls or contract negotiations could have pulled that off. They just had to be there.

We ran into intermittent system problems just before testing began. The drive team in New York was sure it was a media problem, and the Engineers in San Diego were equally convinced it was the hardware. Discussing it by phone one morning, it became clear people weren't communicating. They were defending parochial interests. The New York contingent got on a plane for San Diego that afternoon. By noon the next day, the problem was resolved. Without getting the two groups face-to-face, we could have argued about who was right for months. Instead, we had it resolved in a few hours.

System testing started just after Thanksgiving. It took some extra effort. I remember driving into the plant on Christmas morning to monitor tests. One of the engineers got into trouble with the security people on a weekend. The guards didn't monitor the gate full time on Sunday, since they also inspected the plant. They caught one of the engineers trying to climb in over the gate to work on some tests. It's not often that you find people breaking security rules to get *into* work. As we packed the first cases of completed drives the afternoon of New Year's Eve, we did not want to go home. We were spent, but really energized.

The success of this effort came from many factors, but getting people face-to-face during the challenging moments was pivotal. It kept them focused squarely on the tasks, not distracted with things like complaint sessions or rumors.

Manage the Rumors

Rumors are a daunting challenge for any organization. Wherever there are people, there is an issue of reality. One of the largest schisms between management and workers is the issue of accurate information. Rumors deflect energy from the vision and values.

Leaders become frustrated as rumors ripple through the organization, becoming more menacing as they go. Significant effort is spent on rumor control in groups with low trust. In areas of high trust, people question any discontinuity immediately, so rumors are extinguished before they sap productivity.

The origins of rumors make an interesting study. How do they get started? There are a host of mechanisms, from disgruntled employees trying to stir up trouble to honest mistakes in understanding. Most are the result of idle gossip and curiosity.

I got some insight once when following up after a communication session. I was addressing concerns in my organization during a difficult time. We had been outsourcing work to another plant, and people were unnerved about losing their jobs. I used a "town meeting" format to allay fears and give an opportunity for questions. About half of the people attended the meeting.

After the session, I immediately went to the shop floor to test reactions. When I asked an operator what he thought of the session, he said, "Well, actually I didn't attend but I heard you told everyone we were going to be shut down." I was taken aback because my message was exactly the opposite. The outsourcing effort was completed, and there were no further plans to move volume out. How could someone get the exact opposite message so quickly after the meeting?

This person was not pulling my leg. Through the grapevine, he had gotten the wrong message. Confirmation with several others who got the right message reaffirmed that most people heard my communication correctly. They said the message was crystal clear: no more volume would be leaving the plant.

In an atmosphere of high trust, this kind of misunderstanding is rare, yet it did occur in this instance. This person had no compunction about leveling with me. He was not fearful of any backlash and had been quick to point out issues in the past. Yet he had gotten the wrong information. There was a fascinating phenomenon happening here.

Some people hear what they think you are going to say, even if you say something else. Their predisposition leaves them incapable of absorbing the actual words and meaning. It reminds me of the old Archie Bunker quote, when he says to his wife, Edith, "The reason you don't understand me, is because I'm talking in English and you're listening in Dingbat!"

If people you are trying to reach are worried about some draconian action, it may color their thinking enough to render them effectively deaf. That is why communicating strictly at the head level is dangerous. Test for understanding often, repeat the key points several times, and make sure everyone understands at the gut level. Use visuals to emphasize key points that might be misunderstood.

Imagine the problems in areas where trust levels are low to begin with, and people are afraid to say anything. It is easy to see how rumors germinate. Once started, they tend to multiply and change direction as misinformation zaps around like laser beams in a hall of mirrors. Before long, you are blinded with problems coming from every direction. It can be a huge problem.

When people believe something, *it is real for them,* even though it may not be factual. Once a rumor reaches a critical mass, management is forced to do damage control ***as if the dreaded consequence imagined was actually happening.*** The rumor creates a significant distraction. Handling entrenched rumors requires lots of communication and a return to the fundamental principles of the business. If things are really out of control, get everyone together and discuss the issues openly. It will be a difficult meeting, but it may help clear the air.

In areas of low trust, denials by management only pour kerosene on the fire. It becomes a vicious cycle until it passes or some other rumor moves in to take its place. Often rumors have a date associated with them. You hear statements like, "I got it from a reliable source that there will be a 25% layoff announced this Friday." Once Friday has passed, the rumor dies immediately. Rumors without a date are more difficult to kill.

The best way to deal with rumors is never let them start. That is not easy, but it is a good goal. Having the entire organization grounded in the values, vision, and mission is good preventive medicine because it enables people to see potential disconnects more clearly. This allows them to be dealt with immediately before the laser beams of misinformation start reflecting.

The way to mitigate existing rumors is to squelch them as early as possible. The best defense is to place a high value on open dialog. Reinforce people who bring forth issues or problems. Let the trust grow as a result of that reinforcement. If people know it is safe and rewarding to bring up scary stuff, they will have less need to spread rumors.

Be credible at all times. If you can't give a frank answer because you are sworn to secrecy, then say so. Being cagey will backfire. People will know, and your reputation will suffer. Not being upfront with people creates a huge trust withdrawal. If you can't give an answer, admit it and let the person know why. Covey put it this way:

> "When individuals are duplicitous, when they say one thing but practice another, or when they bad-

> talk people behind their backs but sweet-talk them to their face, there is a subtle but eloquent communication that undermines trust and, inevitably, leads to win-lose agreements and arrangements requiring external supervision, control and evaluation."

Finally, remember the lesson outlined above. Make sure your communications are not ambiguous. Test for understanding often. Be redundant with the key points – perhaps reinforcing your words with an overhead slide or even a handout. Even though the information in my "town meeting" was technically correct, I had failed to communicate with precision. There were probably other times I failed the same way but never knew because it was not tested.

Read Between the Lines

The majority of feedback on your leadership performance, especially if it's negative, will come between the lines, not explicitly or literally. You need to develop a sixth sense for sniffing out signals and decoding them. Reading body language well is a good way to accomplish this.

Look for *changes* in conditions that may relate back to you. If a normal behavior pattern has shifted recently, it is worth checking. To illustrate, here are a few examples of changes you could encounter:

- You might become aware of a strategy meeting at a level you would normally attend. This time you were left off the invitation list without explanation. You checked with the administration person, who acted a little flustered and said that's what "they" wanted.
- Suppose you typically get a complementary note from your boss after your monthly "town meeting" but haven't received one for the past three events. There doesn't seem to be a specific issue, but the support level has shifted. It

could be an overload condition with your boss or a mild signal that you are out of favor.

- You might catch a couple managers chatting in the lunchroom. Out of the corner of your eye, you notice they were looking at you but looked away quickly when you saw them.

- You notice a group of people huddled in the work area and, as you get closer to the group, they quickly disperse back to their work. As you talk to each one, they appear friendly and have no specific complaints, but they also seem a bit cool and somber.

- You notice that a close peer has started sitting farther away from you during staff meetings. You and he have previously enjoyed some interesting sidebar conversations that are no longer possible. It could be you need a new deodorant, or it could be an indication of a subtle rift caused by something you said or did. Another explanation is the boss might have gotten to your friend, asking that you two knock off the sidebar discussions. Check into it.

- You have a topic important to you that has been placed last on the agenda for the past several staff meetings. Time ran out and your agenda item has been rescheduled for a future date.

- You find out from your financial analyst that the boss wants to do an extra review of your year-to-date numbers. You didn't get a call directly from the boss on this.

Don't become consumed with this kind of detective work and get paranoid. Just keep alert to things that don't seem to fit and do some investigating when you spot them. Often the reason is just some random issue that will blow over. If a pattern emerges, bring it up delicately, find out what you are doing wrong, and deal with it.

Excellent communication is never more important than during any kind of transition. Helping people deal with change is a critical leadership function. A good rule of thumb is to at least double your communication efforts when you are in transition.

One of the most challenging transitions is when an incumbent leader moves out of a position and a new leader takes over. Special care is required to keep the organization focused during this time. I will cover these issues thoroughly in Chapters 8 and 10.

Chapter 6 - Style

Style is a fascinating part of leadership. It covers a vast territory, everything from how you react when angered to how you comb your hair. ***Style has a significant impact on trust*** because it defines how you react under certain conditions. If trust is all about consistency, then a deep understanding of your style can help you avoid unwitting trust withdrawals. That doesn't mean your style must be stagnant. It should evolve over time and be tested in various ways discussed later in this chapter. Conscious changes in style need to happen with care so trust is not compromised in the process.

Understand your Style

Webster defines style as, "the distinguishing way in which something is done, said, written, made, executed, etc." How you react to people and situations is the basis of your style. It is also helpful to think of style as an art, and mastery of it will help you interact with other people constructively. Your style will be different under a variety of circumstances. It is a complex area that requires an investment of time to master.

You can characterize your own style and work with others to understand their styles. Once everyone is comfortable with the process, then it can be exciting to work together to optimize how people's styles work together. This improves personal bonding, while reducing friction among your team in daily activities. Do this as an exercise whenever you inherit a new team or want to improve relationships in an existing group. You will learn how to work together more effectively. The process is simple.

Using Style Instruments:

1. Select an instrument that helps characterize style (see below).
2. Have everyone on the team take the survey.
3. Analyze the data with the help of a trained professional.
4. Discuss the implications of style differences.
5. Clarify how you can use these data to improve team effectiveness and interpersonal relations.
6. Develop a plan and get commitment.

Since there are thousands of dimensions, how do you characterize a person's style? There are a number of excellent, well-documented, instruments available that make the task manageable. I will mention two famous ones here, but there are numerous others available through consultants or online under "management style indicators."

A well-known and much-used tool for this purpose by Isabel Briggs-Myers and Katherine Cook Briggs, called the "Myers-Briggs Type Indicator", is available at www.mbti.com. It is based on the work of Dr. Carl Jung, a protégé of Sigmund Freud.

Myers-Briggs creates a 4x4 array, looking at four dichotomies:

Extraversion/ Introversion	How you are energized and focus attention
Sensing/Intuition	How you gather information
Thinking/Feeling	How you decide things
Judging/Perceiving	How you deal with the world

Through an extensive set of questions you identify preferences on the 4 dichotomies and their relative strength. Your style is matched to one of sixteen categories in the 4x4 array. Each of these has a set of characteristics associated with it. Studying your dominant style helps you recognize your patterns of behavior. More importantly, understanding the style of others helps decode certain built-in conflicts between individuals. The instrument is helpful because it prescribes ways to deal with people having different styles.

The Myers-Briggs indicator has high validity with data on thousands of people going back more than 50 years. It allows you to compare your preference data to other people's easily, with no distortion. It increases your self-awareness for the purpose of getting along with others more effectively. It also allows you to identify the source of problems in relationships.

Another useful analytical tool is the DiSC profile based on the theories of Dr. William Marston.

The two dimensions of Dr. Marston's model are:

- The environment is perceived as favorable or unfavorable.
- The individual perceives himself or herself as more or less powerful in that environment.

The DiSC instrument measures behavior patterns based on a four quadrant model as follows:

Dominance	High self-confidence, forcefulness, competitiveness
Influencing	Talkativeness, enthusiasm, optimism, energy
Steadiness	Friendliness, co-operation, persistence, patience
Compliance	Accuracy, caution, concern for high standards

Each of these is given a score and you view a profile of your dominant behaviors based on a specific job. Many consulting groups use DiSC as a starting point and then add more content to broaden the analysis.

Target Training International, Ltd. adds a set of attitudes to the behavior model as follows:

Traditional	The value of tradition, unity and order
Theoretical	The discovery of truth
Utilitarian	The use of money and what is useful
Individualistic	The value of power
Aesthetic	Interest in form and harmony
Social	Love of people

The instrument generates a profile of your strength in each dimension, calculates a comparison of your data with the national population, and presents a statistical graph for each dimension showing if you are:

Mainstream - within one standard deviation of the national mean
Passionate - two standard deviations above the mainstream
Indifferent - two standard deviations below the national mean
Extreme - three standard deviations from the national mean

This is useful because it shows your profile and the strength of each element compared to a broad population. This level of detail allows specific dialog between individuals to increase understanding.

Other instruments have different dimensions but the method is similar. You answer questions about yourself and the instrument places you somewhere in n-dimensional space where n = the number of variables used in that particular instrument.

I like to visualize style as a continuum of many variables, where you display preferences and *manage them* based on the circumstances. There are no wrong or right styles, but how you manifest preferences is critical to success.

Ten examples of dimensions that relate to style:

1. Level of trust	Reinforcing people for sharing conflicting views
2. Political acumen	Knowing when to stand firm and when to back off
3. Emotion vs. Analysis	Dealing with situations - gut level vs. logic
4. Tolerance vs. Impatience	Cracking down or encouraging
5. Irrationality and Fear	Using these or avoiding them
6. Do outrageous things to make a point	Creating folk tales about yourself
7. Dealing with bureaucracy	Feeding the animal when necessary
8. Level of micro-management	Managing by looking over people's shoulders
9. Atmosphere	Having fun in the organization – laughing at ourselves
10. Reinforcement	Making it work as intended

Thinking of style in this context, you can identify additional items for your situation. There is no such thing as a "correct" set of items, but it is helpful to have a list like those above to increase understanding.

Optimizing Leadership Style

Use the list above as a way to generate dialog among your leadership team. How well are you doing with these issues of style? What is working for you and what is not? Each leader has methods of getting through to people, eliciting responses helpful to the organization. Often these style behaviors are occurring on a subconscious level, where the leader is not even aware of how she is responding. It is helpful to have a forum with other leaders where you can share ideas about style and compare notes. These discussions can be pithy, deep, and very insightful. Try taking your key leaders off site for a day or two to discuss these concepts. They will come away refreshed and stimulated.

Allow yourself to explore reasonable modifications to your style in order to learn new ways of leading. This is key to being a leader in a learning organization. Steven Covey described it this way in "Principle-Centered Leadership":

> "Some may wonder if it's possible for senior managers, old dogs, to learn a new style or trick. Some may contend that our styles – whether we are vocalists, comedians, or managers – are so deeply imprinted that by the time we turn ten, twenty, or thirty, they're etched in stone. I think that although it is very difficult to adapt or change our style, it's not impossible. Our leadership style can be 'situational,' but before we're able to make a change, we may require new mentors and models."

One leader may be highly successful using an occasional tantrum, while the same technique would backfire for others. The idea of experimenting with style to learn new modes of operation will enhance your leadership. You cannot change your underlying nature, but there are numerous ways to modify style in particular situations to expand your repertoire.

One caution: develop an environment of trust *before* experimenting with style. If you try different styles without first establishing trust, people will become totally confused, and you will undermine efforts to build the right environment. Your behaviors need to form a pattern of consistency before you can venture into a learning mode on style. When you do, the style must be congruent with your true feelings. You are not playing games with people, only trying a different mode of sharing your feelings. If people react with, "What the heck is he trying to do? He is completely off the wall!" you are too inconsistent. The reaction you are looking for is, "That's interesting. He is not acting with his typical response on this issue. Something significant must be going on here."

Real World Examples

In the living laboratory of leadership I encouraged all leaders to understand their style, solidify it, then grow by trying new approaches. I tried modifying my own style too. This was a fun and easy way to learn new modes of style that helped me broaden skills in several areas. Here are a couple examples for clarity.

I hate customer complaints. They are an intolerable failure of the system and must be totally eliminated. When we would get a complaint, I would insist on an analysis of the failure and corrective actions. I especially hated mixed or misidentified product, where the customer thought they were getting Product A but found Product B in the box. My style, when we got a complaint, was great disappointment followed by firm resolve and ultimately gratitude for the good detective and preventive effort put forth by the staff.

Once when we sent out some product with incorrect packaging, I decided to modify my normal style and become more intense. I became visibly angry, insisting that the people involved call customers to personally warn them and apologize. They got the message and things became tighter after that. Also, the workers got a kick out of talking to real customers. The customers were impressed that factory workers would care enough to pick up the phone to warn them of a potential problem. It worked out well for everyone, and it would never have happened without a willingness to experiment with actions outside my normal style.

Another time, we had something mysterious causing a customer defect. We knew it was caused in our production line but couldn't pinpoint the source. My normal style is to be supportive and patient with the analysis phase, but this time people weren't attacking the problem with enough intensity. I put my sleeping bag in my car and went into the plant to stay until the problem was resolved. That made a big impression and we got to the bottom of it quickly.

That episode also taught me it is vital to verify information *yourself.* The defect consisted of blue spots on the product that were so small they could only be observed under magnification. A technician was assigned to inspect test sheets for spots. He reached the conclusion there was no pattern to the spots, which made diagnosis more difficult. I believed the technician because he was a former quality inspector familiar with this kind of defect. We struggled for days trying to characterize the source with little progress. Finally, at one point, I picked up the magnifier myself and looked intently at the sheet. The technician was correct; the larger of the spots were random. Looking more carefully, I saw there were many extremely small particles that did form a pattern. Once we knew that, the source of contamination was easy to determine.

In "The Contrarian's Guide to Leadership," Steven Sample explained it this way:

> "I call this 'counting the widgets in the stockroom yourself.' It's amazing how often you'll find that the allegedly factual information you've been receiving for years about a particular matter is completely erroneous, not because the person gathering the information is malicious or incompetent, but simply because he misunderstood what it was he was supposed to count or misinterpreted how he was supposed to count it."

There is nothing magic in these examples. The key is to try new things in certain situations so you can grow. After you have a firm foundation in values and vision and you have established an environment of trust, do not always act the same way. Try out new responses in certain situations to see if they work for you. In the process you will be growing in leadership.

Chapter 7 - Attitudes of Leadership

The attitudes a leader reveals through the daily challenges set the tone for the organization, helping to build an environment of trust. This chapter deals with Strength and Courage, Positive Outlook and Passion for Performance.

Strength and Courage

It is a common misunderstanding that good leadership is happening when things are going smoothly. Being "in control" is felt to be the result of a well-executed process brought about by good leaders. People look to leaders to bring stability and security in an uncertain world.

Ironically, the best leaders are incredible destabilizing forces. They are not satisfied being in control. They constantly try to move us out of our complacency or comfort zone. That makes good leaders unpopular at times. The best ones care more for what the organization can do and where it's going than what makes everyone feel good now. Tichy summarized this as follows:

> "...if the marketplace or other external forces don't create problems or opportunities, the leaders do it themselves by breaking down comfortable old structures, setting stretch goals and challenging people to rise to a new level of expectations. They do this because winning leaders understand that times of transition are 'teachable moments,' when most people are most likely to respond because they feel they must. So they create 'burning platforms,' and then help people figure out where and how to jump."

Colin Powell provided an outstanding list of 18 key points on leadership in his "Primer on Leadership." His first point is: "Being responsible sometimes means pissing people off," yet most of us associate good leadership with being popular. Powell notes, "Trying to get everyone to like you is a sign of mediocrity."

You cannot score well in most corporate leadership assessments unless you are well liked. Many of them are approval surveys of subordinates. The corporate culture often associates lack of problems and having everyone happy with good leadership. In most companies the advancement and compensation of leaders is tied to leadership surveys, which reinforce mediocrity because they place a premium on harmony. Companies that evaluate leaders on a holistic basis and reward the best regardless of their current popularity will attract and retain the best leaders.

Marvin was a leader who advanced to a high level by trying to make people feel good all the time. He would bend the truth and finesse every situation to avoid conflict and make people feel good in the moment. He reinforced people with soothing words, even when they were doing poorly. This person was popular and scored well on the leadership assessments, but he was a marginal leader. People tended to discount his praise, because they knew his penchant for avoiding conflict and did not trust him. Powell points out, "Ironically by procrastinating on the difficult choices, by trying not to get anyone mad, and by treating everyone equally 'nicely' regardless of their contribution, you'll simply ensure that the only people you'll wind up angering are the most creative and productive people in the organization."

It would be foolish for you to go around intentionally making people angry. No leader can afford to alienate people unnecessarily, but don't let popularity stand in the way of doing what needs to be done. This is one of the toughest lessons to learn, especially if the organization tends to promote and compensate based on popularity.

Don't get the idea that everything needs to be smooth all the time and everyone needs to be deliriously happy for you to be an outstanding leader. It isn't so. Many leaders who consistently run a smooth ship are surprised when another person who has blundered into disaster, but recovered well, passes them by. A calm stable environment helps reduce the tendency toward ulcers but it does not allow you to exercise your creative leadership muscles. A great leader takes risks, knowing that occasionally there will be problems, but that problems are really opportunities. Bennis writes: "Leaders learn by leading, and they learn best by leading in the face of obstacles. As weather shapes mountains, so problems make leaders."

Great leaders are at their best in a crisis. This is when people need the guidance of a strong leader the most. History is full of examples where leaders who were considered marginal rose to become strong and charismatic in times of crisis. A perfect example is President George W. Bush following the bombing of the World Trade Center on September 11, 2001. Before the attack, many viewed him as an ex-party-boy without much leadership strength. Within a week of the disaster, the majority of Americans viewed him as one of the strongest presidents in modern times. That is a huge turn-around in a single week. History may not sustain the gain, but that is not the point. Crisis times are real opportunities for leaders.

When you feel most vulnerable or threatened as a leader is often the time when you have the greatest opportunity to shine. Properly managed, these situations enhance your reputation rather than destroy it. Therefore, take heart in times of crisis, and stick by your values and convictions. Remain resolute, focused, and flexible. Look at the situation from all angles. Do not panic but move quickly to take charge, and people will follow your lead. Use the energy created by the crisis to direct people toward the goal rather than be scattered to the wind. Tichy wrote, "winning leaders transform negative energy into positive energy…they harness the energy that is generated in times of distress so that their organizations not only survive difficulties that destroy other institutions, but emerge stronger for the experience."

Lead people through the crisis with courage. Your superiors will notice and you will have advanced your reputation as a good leader. The bigger the disaster, the greater the opportunity to shine. As Yogi Berra put it, "To get maximum attention, it's hard to beat a good, big mistake."

Fletcher Byrum, former president of Coopers, wrote a list of "commandments" for people who aspire to be great leaders. His last point read, "Make sure you generate enough mistakes – that's right, make sure you generate enough mistakes."

Obviously, it is not a good idea to carry the logic to extreme. If you go around intentionally creating disasters so you can clean them up, you are headed for trouble.

It takes fortitude to be a good leader. Often, it requires being the champion of unpopular initiatives. The ability to sell unpleasant but necessary activities requires strength and courage.

Weaker leaders tend to blame others for a difficult-to-sell program. They will say "I do not agree with this, but we have to do it because it's mandated from above." This goes back to the desire to be a popular leader. In reality, it weakens a leader's position with superiors and doesn't fool subordinates. This is a trustbuster. It takes real courage to acknowledge there were other choices, but we are going to take a tough route and make it work.

The ability to demonstrate strength is derived from a deep respect that is rooted in credibility. The leader must be highly credible or people will harpoon the initiative. That credibility can only occur in an environment of high trust.

People go to great lengths to avoid disappointing a strong leader. The respect is so apparent, they would do anything to keep from letting the leader down. This is easily confused with strength due to fear. Hitler convinced thousands of soldiers to commit atrocities they would not consider normally. For most, this was not out of respect, but out of fear. ***Great leaders eliminate fear and install trust in its place.***

Every day leaders make tough calls, some of which will be unpopular. The leader needs the fortitude to go against the grain if that is required. This toughness can be found in many decision areas such as:

> Who are the right people to lead the organization?
> How do you discipline with fairness and compassion?
> Should we grow or shrink the organization?
> What size staff is necessary to support our business?
> When should we exit a business?
> How do we manage scarce resources – money, talent, equipment, etc.?

The list could go on, as there are hundreds of areas where leaders make tough calls. Great leaders don't shy away from controversy; they realize it is why they are called leaders. The best ones make courageous decisions within a *framework* that guarantees the decisions are the best ones under the circumstances. A typical example of such a framework would look like the following list.

A Framework for Making Tough Calls

1. Always operate from a set of values. Test every action and decision to determine consistency with the values and the vision.
2. Do an assessment laying out the facts.
3. Don't operate in a vacuum. Get input from the people impacted, but do not let the will of the masses dictate the decision.
4. Develop a list of potential decisions, and test the validity and impact of each.
5. Assess support for the decision in advance, and do whatever possible to gain support if it will be unpopular.
6. Act swiftly and decisively, avoiding the "analysis paralysis" problem.
7. Communicate the decision and rationale with high energy, and listen carefully to the feedback.
8. Commit wholly to the decision, and don't waffle if there is resistance. Admit ownership of the decision. Do not blame someone else.
9. Continually evaluate the impact, and have the courage to admit if it was a mistake.

This framework ensures progress toward the vision, while preserving the environment of trust, even if the decision is necessarily unpopular.

Decisions involving placement of people are more difficult than business decisions. Especially challenging is identifying who should lead in an organization. Chapter 9 deals with these issues.

Positive Outlook

Exceptional leaders constantly display a positive outlook with incredible energy and drive. They may get angry or energized, but they are rarely depressed because there is no time for it. They are too busy making lemonade out of the lemons they encounter. It almost seems like a game as these people absorb tremendous setbacks and just reset the course to be successful anyway. The great marketing guru, Ted Nicholas, admits he has more failures in his advertisements than successes. Whenever one fails, rather than get discouraged, he simply says "next," and generates another try for success. Though his batting average is below 500, he has enough "at bats" to hit plenty of home runs.

There is an infectious enthusiasm for the vision of a true leader. Because this vision is rooted in core values and describes a pathway toward an exciting future, people identify with it and climb aboard emotionally. The leader's vision is so compelling that it surfaces in every speech or conversation. Every decision supports his vision. This is why people rally behind him. The vision is positive and compelling. Warren Bennis in "Managing People is like Herding Cats" said, "Almost all leaders are purveyors of hope. Their optimism fascinates me because it is so pervasive and so powerful. I don't think it can be built on phony grounds either."

Good leaders have a Pollyanna approach to adversity. As problems arise, they are promptly put in the "challenges to overcome" category, just another mountain to climb on the way to the vision. If carried to extreme, this can annoy some people who have a need to worry (or, as they would describe it, "the need to be more realistic.") They want to stew over the "what ifs" that loom on the horizon, but the leader takes them in stride as a normal part of risk management. There is a strong belief in the team and its ability to charge through any obstacle. Don't assume everyone else shares your optimism. It is healthy to have different levels of worry in an organization. This diversity creates a balance allowing high momentum with the right mix of caution and preventive damage control.

All groups tend to vent at times. It is human nature to complain about conditions, deadlines, bureaucracy, budgets, resources, etc. Some groups are world-class at venting. If there is a 2-hour meeting, you can count on more than 100 minutes of griping and venting. That's a bad habit found in groups at all levels and disciplines.

Great leaders put a stop-loss on the bitching. They allow a certain amount to bleed off pressure, but then refocus the dialog along more constructive lines. Rather than focus on what is wrong, they prefer to spend time on what needs to be done now. Lou Holtz said, in his famous video titled "Do Right," "You just have to focus on what's important now. The rest will take care of itself."

One trick is to set a time limit for venting. If people are stressed out and need to complain, allow five minutes for it, then move to more constructive dialog. This simple technique saves hours of unconstructive griping. Another idea is to have a pot of money in the room. If someone gets caught bitching without a constructive suggestion, they have to put a dollar in the pot. This is funny at first, but after people have to get change for a $20 bill, they quit venting. Making a decision to move groups quickly from venting to constructive ideas is a hallmark of good leadership.

Optimism carries more energy than pessimism, and energy is needed to scramble after tough goals. Become a role model for keeping groups from despair. Take the high road whenever you can and, if someone accuses you of wearing rose colored glasses, just say, "Thank you – the world is a much more enjoyable place with them." Carried to an extreme, it can become a problem, but for most people, a shift toward a more optimistic outlook will improve their leadership.

Passion for Performance

Great leaders are passionate people. They have a perpetual fire in the belly for their goals and vision. They show by deeds and words that they will not be deterred from their mission.

In the work setting, great leaders are passionate about *performance*. They know how to translate urgency into positive action. Contrast this with poor leaders who get all excited about the need to do better but can't translate it well to people. They use all kinds of exhortations, even threats. There is much arm waving and gum flapping, but it does not connect with people. Why? There is little passion, just frantic excitement! The real leader has a different intensity, one that does not require loud rhetoric or threats because it is backed up with demonstrable passion from within. It is the smoldering white-hot fire of true resolve that people recognize and follow. While the poor leader practically shouts words in rapid succession, the true leader often talks in low volume with a slow deliberate cadence.

The passionate leader becomes energized in the face of problems. Rather than hoping for some miracle to make things better, energy is focused on solving the problem. The real kick is found in performing beyond expectations. She inspires people to routinely do things they never dreamed possible, creating winners. People catch the infectious enthusiasm and ride it like a racehorse from one victory to another. Problems and setbacks are merely hurdles to be crossed with care.

Passionate leaders are more than involved. They are totally committed to excellence. For them, nothing less will satisfy. The brass ring is what they seek and what they must have.

Jack Welch of General Electric placed a high value on passion. He modeled it himself and took every opportunity to instill it among the people. His frequent visits to GE's institute at Crotonville, often called "the Harvard of corporate America," would stress this. In his book, "jack: Straight from the Gut" he put it this way:

> "Whenever I went to Crotonville and asked a class what qualities define an 'A player,' it always made me happiest to see the first hand go up and say, 'Passion.' For me, intensity covers a lot of sins. If there's one characteristic all winners share, it's that they care more than anyone else. No detail is too small to sweat or too large to dream. Over the years, I've always looked for this characteristic in the leaders we selected. It doesn't mean loud or flamboyant. It's something that comes from deep inside. Great organizations can ignite passion."

Leaders with high passion reinforce in a different pattern. They focus on performance as well as behaviors. They view the potential for performance improvement as nearly infinite. No matter how remarkable the improvements made today, we are hardly scratching the surface of what is possible. That makes for a pretty exciting world, one worth pursuing. It also constitutes a competitive advantage over organizations whose leaders believe they have improved productivity as much as possible. You might hear a leader say, "We have made double digit productivity improvements for the past 5 years and we really can't expect any more from this area." Nonsense. The group may have reached a temporary plateau, but there are probably huge productivity gains – orders of magnitude - still available.

In our quality work, we did an exercise on breaking paradigms to illustrate this. We would have a group of 20-30 people form a circle. One person would throw a ball to another person across the circle, then, from that person to a third and so on, until everyone had caught the ball once. Everyone was to remember who was throwing him the ball and who would catch it next. After this "dry run," the group did it again. This time we would time how long it took the ball to touch everyone in the prescribed order. Generally it would take 30-45 seconds to complete the circuit.

At this point, we told the group they could make any changes they wanted and start over. The only condition was that the ball had to go from one person to another in the exact same order. We asked the group to predict the ultimate best time for the exercise. At this point estimates of best time would range from 15-25 seconds. No one ever guessed it could be done in less than 10 seconds.

We allowed the group to brainstorm ideas and repeat the process. A typical idea was to arrange everyone in order so the ball could go from one to another without traveling very far. That would knock at least 50% off the time. We let the group brainstorm more and kept repeating the process until they believed they had gone as far as possible. No group had a final result above 3 seconds. One group had a measured time of less than 0.1 second! They each extended their index finger and arranged the fingertips in a helix pattern so the ball would touch each finger in the right order as it was dropped instantly through the helix.

The productivity improvements seen in this example were orders of magnitude greater than the most optimistic estimates at the start. It showed that humans grossly underestimate the level of improvement opportunities.

Lean Manufacturing work has an activity called Kaizen, where a team will focus on a process for 4-5 days and normally improve productivity 25% to 50% in that single week. The same group can go back again to improve another double-digit percentage in another week. The level of improvement is nearly infinite, and it typically dwarfs any reasonable estimate made beforehand. Multiply the conventional wisdom of maximum potential improvement for any process by 10. That may approach the actual limit of improvement available.

This is why great leaders are passionate about improving performance. They know it is possible and are excited to make it reality.

Great leaders accomplish much in organizations through demonstration of three key attitudes. They are not afraid to model strength and courage, especially during the most difficult times. Their outlook is always positive and focused on the brass ring. Finally, they have a magical way of transmitting their personal passion throughout the organization.

We have described how to establish a firm foundation for the business and build an environment of trust. We have discussed the key factors of excellent leadership. It is now time to pull this together into a real-world context and allow the genius of leadership to make good and lasting change in the organization.

SECTION TWO
Chapter 8 - Change Essentials

It is abundantly true that change is the only constant. Improvement initiatives are ubiquitous in business. Each one takes significant energy and expense, but is supported gladly by management because it has a high expected payback. Sadly, the majority of these fall short of the desired outcome and many end up as failures. The investment is squandered; morale and productivity suffer.

Since change is inevitable, ensure that any investment has a real payback and actually exceeds advertised benefits. Establish the right *environment* for change. Start by recognizing a well-known but little heeded axiom: "Change done to me is scary, but change done by me is energizing."

The first rule of effective change is involvement of impacted people in planning, executing, and celebrating the change effort. Let's start by examining the leader's role.

The leader must be passionate about change. She must be the prime motivator for the effort and enroll the entire management team in it. She must put her shoulder into the activity with her time and energy. This is no place to delegate to an underling or hire a consultant, as many leaders do. That sends a terribly wrong signal. A consultant may assist in design or execution, but should never be viewed as the focal point. The leader must see this as the prime agenda for improvement and not let it compete with several other programs. Underlings and various teams will carry out much of the culture-changing work, but without the passionate resolve of the leader, the effort is doomed.

Four Stages of Change

Adapted from: K. Buckley & D. Perkins in J. Adams' "Transforming Work"; Alexandria, VA: Miles River, 1984

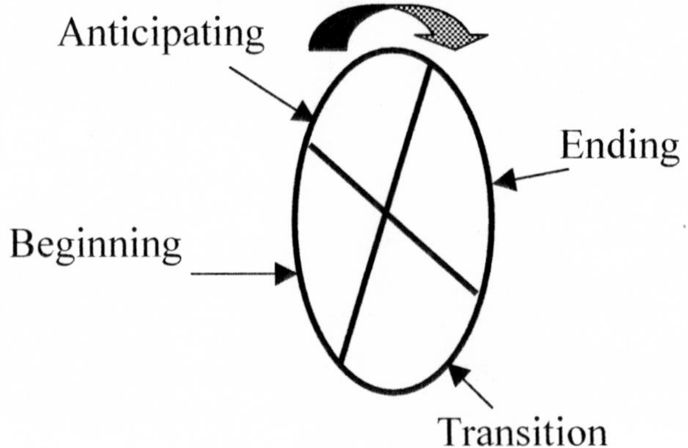

A Change Model

The process of change will go more smoothly if people understand the psychology of change. I like a business adaptation of grief counseling, where reacting to change is broken into four segments: Anticipating, Ending, Transition, and Beginning.

Anticipating

This is the "fat, dumb and happy" state in the old paradigm. You are scarcely aware of the impending need for change. Ultimately, through some hints, you become aware of a threat to the old way of being. Denial is typical at this point. You hope the problem will go away and that your invested stake in the current paradigm is safe. For example, in the late 1960's, managers at Dietzgen Company, makers of slide rules, must have felt that way when Hewlett Packard introduced the new handheld calculators.

Ending

A new beginning requires that something must end. In this phase, you become fearful of loss. You see a necessity to move out of your comfort zone and that's scary. People often become sad or depressed in this phase and feel helpless, knowing a change is occurring, but longing for the days when the old ways sustained them. This phase is often compared to a death and, frequently, in the corporate world, it is a death. People need to grieve for what is ending. Leaders who understand and compassionately assist in this grief process enable the change to move more quickly. By allowing people to acknowledge their pain and express it, the leader gently moves people toward the next phase. Those who don't, pay a large price later in lack of commitment or other negative consequences. This is one area where overdoing the positive outlook, discussed in the previous chapter, can cause resentment.

Transition

This is the chaos and turmoil normally associated with change. In this phase, people jockey for a better position in the new paradigm. Bargaining or rationalizing is common in the form of: "If we have to move to a different building, at least can I get a bigger office or a closer parking space?" Rumors and speculation abound in this phase and information management becomes a real issue. Often anger or hostility are displayed in the transition as people, finally resolved to their fate, lash out at the injustice of it. Some still manifest denial of the transition, while others choose sides in the political chaos. During the transition, the leader's skill is most needed and most tested. There needs to be clear focus on the vision as people deal with the confusion and let go of the past.

Beginning

Finally people begin to accept the new way. When you build stake in the new processes, people enroll, sometimes with delight and sometimes begrudgingly. Slowly the team begins to rebuild enthusiasm and eventually starts performing in the new paradigm.

People need to understand these phases because, with that knowledge, and the skill of a good leader, the time to make the full transition can be shortened. For example, I have seen teams make it through a difficult change that normally would take 6 months in about 6 days because they were aware and managing the phases. It helps people to know the grief they feel in the ending stage will be followed by better days. They tend to arrive at the transition more quickly. Also, if they realize that the anger experienced in transition is normal, something that needs to be vented, it becomes less distracting. That is a huge advantage because it allows some stability in the new paradigm before the need for another change is evident. Groups that are efficient at getting through the steps have a natural competitive advantage.

Foundations & Pursuit of Vision

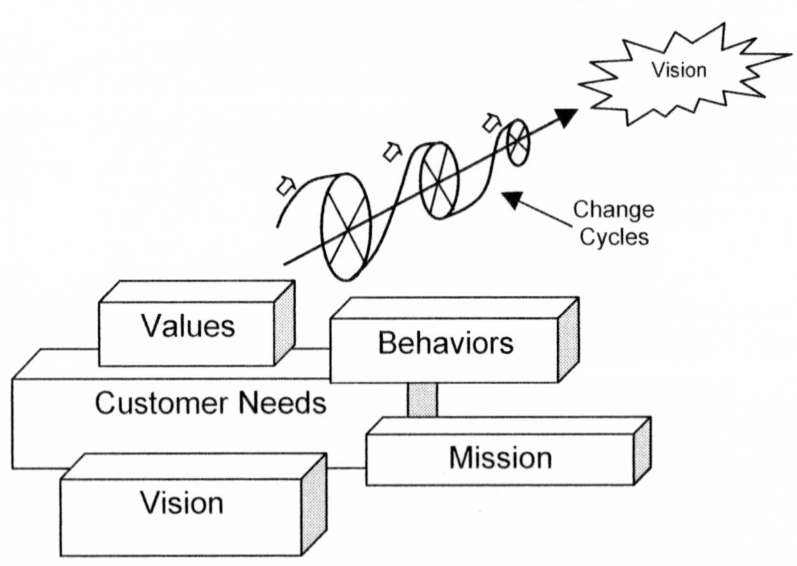

A helpful way to view the change process is shown above. You have a solid foundation based on the concepts outlined in Chapter 2. The stages of change are like the ellipses where each cycle goes through anticipating, ending, transition and beginning. This is followed by a period of stability before the next change cycle begins. As the team becomes more adept at handling change, the ellipses become more compact because the team goes through the stages more quickly. This allows more time for sustained performance between change cycles. People appreciate that and perform better.

There are several other factors necessary for successful change initiatives. If you have them in place, change efforts will go smoothly. Great leaders make sure the following conditions are achieved ***before*** attempting a restructuring or culture change.

Essential Requirements for Successful Change

High Trust

Having an environment of high trust is essential during change processes because it allows everyone to contribute without fear. If people know they can voice their grief or anger without retribution, they will be more willing to enroll in the change effort. High trust also allows leaders to tap into the diversity of ideas that are present in any group since everyone feels open. That adds to the quality and creativity of problem solutions and higher buy-in among all people. *They* own the change.

Methods of establishing a high trust environment were covered in Chapter 4.

Tolerance for Risk

Another condition for successful change is tolerance for risk. No progress is made without some risk of failure. If people believe they will be crucified for doing something, they will be reluctant to take the bold steps needed. The leader must keep an eye on the big picture. There are bound to be setbacks along the way. Plan on them and don't come unglued when they show up.

Assess the risks and take preventive measures to mitigate potential problems. In some cases, a formal backup plan might be wise if there is a particularly risky new procedure. For example, when cutting over to a new parts supplier, keep the old supplier active until all potential problems are resolved. Otherwise, you could lose the whole business while trying to make things better.

Avoid Pitfalls

Improvement initiatives must be undertaken for a specific purpose. Too often there is a "shotgun" approach where someone comes in with a slick package and sells it to management. This becomes the current program, whether it matches the needs perfectly or not. It sounds like something good to do, so management invests time, energy, and money in the program.

Contrast that with the approach now possible because your organization has a solid framework. The gaps become evident as you compare where you are with the vision. Now you can identify a few things most helpful at filling these gaps. These are the linchpins that couple the present reality to the ideal future. Because these are critically needed now, they have a powerful pull throughout the organization.

Getting Everyone Enrolled

People at all levels must be enrolled and support the change initiative. One weak link in the chain can create fatal problems. The danger here is not the people who fully oppose the change and say so. These people can be converted, or their message of opposition may be right. Listen well and debate accordingly. The real danger is the snake-in-the-grass who fully agrees with the initiative outwardly, but does subtle and untraceable things to undermine the process. Leaders need a sixth sense to sniff out people with double agendas and deal with them forthrightly. Chapter 10 covers staffing issues that might arise, including effective ways to remove people with low commitment.

A Burning Platform

Many people need a little push to make the leap to a new and uncomfortable place. For most it is like standing on a diving board looking into the icy water, wondering if they really wanted a swim after all. The well-known "boiled frog" analogy is the best way to describe it.

If you put a frog in a pan of boiling water, it will immediately jump out and, despite some singed feet, will live to croak again. However, if you put a frog in a pan of cool water and slowly add heat, the frog will boil to death because it does not sense the danger until it is too late. Great leaders know this and provide hot water early enough. They find a way to jolt people out of their comfort zone and keep the pressure on until everyone accepts the need for change.

If people understand the gaps between the current state and the vision, they will instinctively generate ideas to close them. As the teams become process owners, real change throughout the organization begins to accelerate.

A Compelling Vision of the Future

If people can't see a better world at the end of the journey, don't expect them to be wild about the process. That's why it is critical to have people at all levels support the vision. Leaders become the artists who carefully paint the picture of a better future on the canvas of today's paradigm. That takes creativity, sincerity and repetition.

Integration of the New Methods into the Existing Culture

Often an embryonic change activity is smashed on the rocks of the old paradigm because it doesn't fit and is rejected by the people. Once you have invented a new policy or procedure, document the change in a user-friendly way and make sure everyone knows that, from now on, this is the way we do things. All new employees need to see how procedures fit into the culture. People need to see the context and how it relates to the vision.

It helps if the change process is a phased project. People know they are in Phase 1 and that the Phase 2 part will be coming next month. They understand context and end goal. New ideas will come up all the time in an environment of trust. If these are integrated so people see how they fit with the current culture, you will not lose momentum. Because the new culture is rooted in the vision and values, it is congruent and has staying power.

Reinforcement of Small Wins along the Way

The journey to the Vision is long and arduous. People cannot maintain the pace without encouragement along the way. A reinforcing culture keeps the energy high enough to persevere during discouraging times.

Chapter 11 covers reinforcement in detail. In times of significant change, continual reinforcement becomes the glue that holds the entire effort together through the process.

Constancy of Purpose over Time

Because change initiatives require so much energy, it is a mistake to roll out new ones too often. People need to get out of the transition and into a sustaining mode to recover their wits before starting a new program. Too often, a new initiative is begun months before the last one is completed. People become disillusioned as they integrate the current project and don't know if last month's rules are suspended or still in effect.

Constancy of purpose is different from constancy of action. You can keep your purpose, but be forced to change how you achieve it. Many companies found themselves having to do this in the wake of 9/11. Purpose and vision enable organizations to flow better with challenges.

The leader helps people understand there will be a series of changes to reach the vision. It's like a massive chess game that goes on over a period of time. People should not expect one single event or initiative to do it all. In the movie, "What About Bob," the psychiatrist played by Richard Dreyfuss prescribed that Bob achieve his vision through a series of "baby steps." That's a great analogy for businesses as well. Hundreds of small, relatively safe steps with lots of encouragement in between are more effective than one huge and risky leap.

Handling Disconnects by Thinking like an Owner

You will need to "sell" your change initiatives up the organization, as well as down. Sometimes it's easier for a middle manager to sell new ideas to subordinates than to management.

Both are equally important. Do your homework before presenting your program to management. Here are a few tips that will help:

- Understand who has to approve your program and find out the political climate.
- Determine the financial implications of your proposal and make sure you have a compelling business case.
- Pre-release information as appropriate to develop allies in support of your proposal.
- Find out if there are competing proposals in other parts of the organization.
- Do a "trial balloon" with the decision maker so you will have a preview of any concerns.
- Determine the best timing and venue to present your plan.

Despite all these efforts, your program may run into some flack or be rejected. If that happens, you may become upset with management. You might reason, "This is a really smart thing to do for the company, but Management won't approve it. They are clueless."

The antidote to this frustration is to start thinking like an owner. Ask yourself some tough questions like, "If this were coming out of my own pocket, would I really be so supportive?" Another good test is to ask, if you had all the shareholders take a proxy on your initiative would it really pass? In smaller programs, you might test if you are proposing this for the good of the company or for personal gain. Finally, test the ethics of the proposal. Is it immoral, illegal, or dumb? If it doesn't fly, it is time to rework the strategy.

Reasons your proposal may be rejected:

- Upper management may not be acting in congruence with stated values, vision and mission, or there may be a disconnect between how you understand these things and how upper management sees them. There may be things you did not take into account during the analysis discussed in Chapter 2. This is a signal to step back, assess the issue, and take a different path forward.

- Your pet project may not be aligned with the true vision as seen by upper management. Keep testing for this. Often, higher-level strategies are not as clear as you would like, or they may be clear but just not valid. If your initiative really fits the stated vision but is still rejected, it is likely that a different, hidden agenda is in effect. In this case you need to tactfully try to identify and resolve the problem with upper management.

- You may have failed to get your initiative well understood up the chain. If you haven't done a good job of selling your initiative, why should management buy into it? Before presenting an idea, think of it as a marketing campaign in your political environment. Find allies and understand your foes. Get input so you can counter any arguments. Thoroughly prepare to do battle for your cause.

- Your idea may be too risky in your current environment. If you propose a new gas pipeline that will save millions of dollars on transportation, but it runs over hostile territory, you may be overlooking a thing or two.

- Timing is another drawback. "This is great but the timing is wrong. Come back in a year."

- Higher priority work may push your project to below the funding cutoff. This is frustrating because everyone agrees the project is great, but "We just don't have enough money to do all the things we want to do." Be prepared to swallow hard and think creatively about how your initiative could be modified to lower costs and raise benefits.

- You might not understand (or be privy to) the bigger picture. Sure, investing in a new boiler could save your plant a lot of money, but if a merger planned for next year makes your building obsolete, it isn't such a "hot" project.

If your initiative is rejected, make sure you find out the real reason. Often the stated reason is a smokescreen. "We like the idea, George, but we want to get the Waterman account firmed up before we think about implementing it." Use all your detective skills to dig beneath the surface and you can usually find the fire under the smoke. A key ally in this could be the staff and administration people closest to the decision-makers.

Foster outstanding relationships with the support staff of people higher in your organization. The administrative assistant or secretary to the big boss is particularly important. Do your best to be empathetic with these people and give praise with gratitude whenever they help you. These people have a lot more power than meets the eye. Here are a few reasons.

How Support People can help you:

- The administrative person holds the key to the boss' calendar. If you are a favored person because of past dealings, you can gain access when others might get bumped. Don't abuse this advantage but cherish it and reinforce the person for any favors.
- Support people have knowledge of the sidebar conversations with the boss. They will overhear things and have useful clues. Integrity will prevent them from giving you information outright, but if you have mastered the art of reading body language, you can know a great deal about the inner workings.
- If support people like you, they will put in a good word for you when it counts the most. The boss, Alice, might say to her secretary, "I think Pete is being really anal about these maintenance reviews. He keeps bugging me about them." The secretary offers, "He really does show a lot of passion for doing things right. If we had more people like him we would be sitting pretty." But the real payoff is that the next time you are in the area, this secretary will pull you aside and tell you, "Alice is starting to get annoyed by your intensity on the maintenance reviews. Keep up the work, but tone down the volume a little." That kind of information is priceless.

- Support people know the published agenda as well as all the unpublished ones. If you are appreciated, they will share the inside scoop inadvertently without loss of integrity. Take them to lunch every once in a while as a "thank you" for their help. Do not pump them for information, but just try to uncover how you can help their situation.

One word of caution, these support people are extremely sensitive about their positional power. Do not "suck up" to them with false praise or lavish gifts, etc. It will backfire. Do not ask them to share information that could compromise their trust with the boss. Trust is a top priority for them, and if you are asking for gossip, you will turn them off immediately. Instead, realize the pressure cooker they are in and be helpful where possible. Just sharing an empathetic ear will help, but reinforcing their actions *sincerely and appropriately* will get you on the right road.

Implementation Issues

Once your change initiative is approved, the work is just beginning. Now you must ensure everyone understands the rationale and supports the program. Start with your close circle of leaders and enroll them all as ambassadors. Each one is needed to translate the impacts into their part of the organization.

Set up a group to oversee the initiative with you in a key position. Any problem of implementation needs to be addressed quickly to avoid loss of momentum. Setbacks are common, but an alert implementation group can usually intervene before damage is done.

Often flaws in a process do not show up until it is being executed. If an initiative backfires despite your best planning efforts, face the situation and immediately make revisions. You do not lose trust admitting a mistake and taking corrective action. You do lose trust trying to push a wrong agenda because you are too proud to admit an error. One word of caution: Often the words used to describe an initiative can get in the way.

"Empowerment" – The Word

Overused words become a problem when their original meaning becomes twisted and obscured. For a time in the mid-nineties, this was the case with the word "empowerment." Originally, it was a helpful way to describe using one's personal power to engage in the business. As managers, consultants, HR, and training personnel started using the word in every imaginable context to describe different things, it became an albatross.

Whenever a manager would say they had a program and they were "going for empowerment," it was time to raise the caution flag. People would ascribe all kinds of meanings to the word that were confusing and detrimental. For example, some people believed empowerment meant everyone got to do what they wanted and nobody was really in charge. Imagine the chaos.

Recently the stigma has worn away and the word can again find a helpful place in our vocabulary. However, the lesson is useful. Be alert for words becoming overused.

Program of the Month

Be sensitive to the word "program" and avoid using it. It is so easy to describe a thrust that includes much training and effort as a program. The subconscious mind interprets this as a short-term thing that can be either ignored or complied with begrudgingly. A more helpful way to describe it is a new dimension – a permanent enhancement to our set of beliefs. If you substitute the word "initiative" for "program," you will be better off.

If you view everything in the context of a learning organization, where people are growing all the time, you can reduce a problem called "program-of-the-month." Programs are started abruptly with great fanfare. Significant time and energy are invested in generating a training program. Trainers use the words "put everyone through the program," which is another red flag. They get engrossed in the training events and measure progress by the percentage of people trained. The progress may be less than hoped. Real progress comes from real change, not attendance rosters.

Often the organization is still in the implementation phase of a current effort when a new improvement program comes along. The old program is not killed off, but is allowed to atrophy as all attention is focused on the new one. The most effective antidote to the program-of-the-month issue is to have an environment of trust. If this exists, people won't allow initiatives to get out of control. If the initiative has many parts, link them together as phases instead of calling each one a separate program.

In "Principle-Centered Leadership," Steven Covey describes it this way:

> "These well intentioned training efforts try to create a spirit of cooperation. But the culture is so polarized, so based on defending positions and coercive power, carrot and stick motivations, that people resist these initiatives. The culture becomes cynical. The next new initiative is perceived as another fruitless, dramatic, desperate, frantic effort to make good things happen. Gradually the culture gets fatigued and demoralized."

The cure is to select improvement efforts with care. Invest in them until the new methods have been fully assimilated into the culture. Then, if there is another effort, make sure it fits well with the previous one. Work hard to demonstrate how these efforts fit synergistically to take you to the vision.

One Size Fits All

Another danger is the "one size fits all" issue. Leaders may become excited about a specific "program." Some may feel it is important for everyone in the organization to get exactly the same training. Others may view it as being thrust upon people, and the effort becomes compromised before it ever starts. For some groups, this training may not be of highest value. A group could be far beyond what is being taught. They may be reluctant to push back because they will not appear as good team players. This is not the best mindset to get maximum benefit from training.

One litmus test is to ask a group to consider skipping a course after they have been scheduled for it. If they push back, indicating how much they will benefit from it, you have a good chance for success. If they turn around, yell "YESSSS!" and start with the "high fives" all around the room, you might want to reconsider. Most people feel overworked in their jobs. Any time allotted for training will result in more work later to catch up on. When people feel a training program is a waste of their time it is easy to detect. Be alert and test for commitment. If it is low, find out why before charging ahead.

There is a better way to manage improvement efforts. First, there must be a strong local ownership for the training. If it is an untargeted, canned program from company headquarters put on by hired facilitators, chances for success are low. If the senior managers really believe in a venture enough to teach it themselves and have their underlings teach it to the next level, it shows an entirely different commitment. When this kind of effort can be tailored to meet the needs of each group as it permeates the organization, you get a win-win scenario.

Putting it all into practice

You have defined your vision, values, and behaviors, developed your own style and strengths, as well as those of your staff. You have built an environment of trust. You understand the dynamics of change and some of the essentials needed to make it work, relating them back to the framework developed in Chapter 2. It is now time to focus on putting all this into practice.

In order to achieve the Vision, three aspects of business must support the process. The organizational structure and staffing must be put in place and developed so they work efficiently. The corporate culture needs to energize and reinforce the qualities that guarantee success. People need the proper training and mentoring to work to their fullest potential, both individually and in teams.

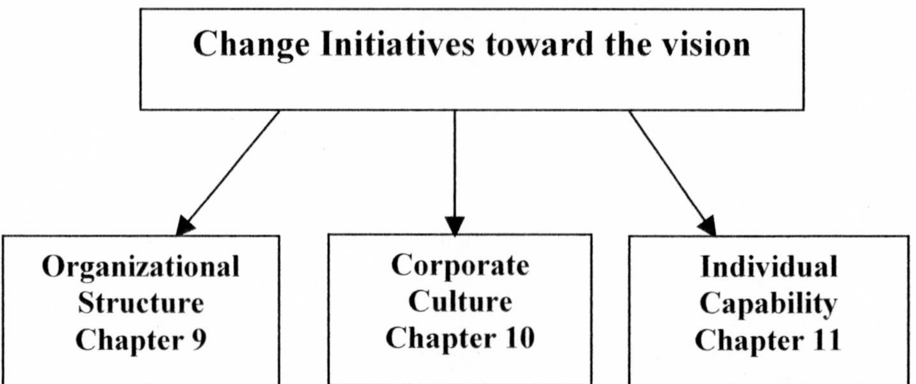

The rest of this book covers these issues which relate to the process of change as shown above.

Chapter 9 - Developing Organizational Structure

This chapter covers organizational issues from three aspects:

1. Creating the structure to support what you want to accomplish.
2. Helping people be effective in a changing environment.
3. Facilitating the transition of leaders. This is a messy topic, since everything is situational. Rather than firm guidelines, we will look at the issues and danger areas. There are no textbook "right" answers. The only right answer is the one you, and your team, develop and are committed to.

No leader operates in a vacuum. All organizations have some kind of structure. Many have abandoned the classical military hierarchy for a more participatory reporting structure. You can find just about any geometric two-dimensional form to depict relationships within an organization. The circle is often used where various groups emanate from a central hub. Ovals describe loosely linked pods of activity. The inverted triangle is an attempt to show the real power is with the people rather than the bureaucracy. This is the "servant leader" concept described by Ken Blanchard and other authors. This view holds that the leader actually reports to the underlings and supports them rather than the reverse. Gareth Morgan in his book, "Imagin-i-zation" offers many creative organizational structures, even comparing organizations to spider plants.

There is always some kind of reporting relationship in play, where some are called to act as formal or informal leaders. The hierarchy may be cleverly disguised as unfocused leadership, but there are reporting relationships in every case.

Most people find themselves in the middle, reporting to someone on a higher level and having others who report to them. All but the very top and bottom have this in common. One can argue the CEO reports to a higher level – the Board of Directors – and the entry level person often has others at home who rely on their leadership. All of us are in a "sandwich," where there are slices above and below. We need to constantly juggle the needs of the other levels while trying to maintain some sanity for ourselves.

The misunderstanding between worker and management is a schism that dilutes the ability of any organization to survive. Each level has the same challenge, trying to interpret guidance from above to those below in a way that does not compromise personal integrity or the needs of the organization. The majority of stress we feel at work is a result of this tension. It is constant, it is mind numbing, and it is everywhere.

This is a great place to test your leadership capability. Outstanding leaders are expert at working the interface between levels. They clarify disconnects upward and interpret decisions downward. They recognize that there is always some tension between the layers, but find ways to keep things under control. Do this consistently and well and you will be among the elite leaders.

Tips to help you improve the interface between levels:

- Thoroughly understand the point of view of layers below you. Listen to input and test for understanding. Be careful to not let the views of the vocal few characterize the beliefs of the silent majority.

- Recognize that many of the desires of levels below you are human nature. What group would not want more pay, more personal freedom, more recognition, more time off, etc. Don't discount these needs, but realize they are universal. Try to find more specific suggestions, and be alert for ideas that can be done without major investment. Often it's the little things that can make a big difference to people.

- Interpreting these needs upward is also an art. Don't be a whiner for your team. Clarify their needs accurately and objectively.
- Internalize the impact of management actions while they are being developed. Make sure top management knows how things will be perceived at lower levels before actions are announced. Avoid sounding negative in these discussions by offering possible alternative decisions or more creative ways of describing them. Ask questions instead of making blunt statements. For example, instead of saying, "They will interpret this as another attempt by management to line their own pockets," you might offer, "Would it be better received if we coupled this announcement with the employee bonus plan?"
- Avoid being a "Chicken Little" in discussions with upper management. Ultimately, you need to support and sell these decisions downward, so work to influence your superiors. Do this from a viewpoint of "what is best for the business," rather than "how to keep the masses from revolting." Senior managers want to do what is best for the organization. They sometimes need help understanding the impact of poor decisions on their own destiny. You can be the voice of reason, but only if you maintain credibility and perspective.

Designing the Organization - Form Follows Function

Your assessment from Chapter 2 should include a close look at your current organization. Based on your framework of values, vision, mission, behaviors, and a strategic plan, you can shape the organization to support them.

The classic hierarchy is neither required nor desired in an empowered organization. The old chain of command must give way to a more streamlined structure. Referring to the SWOT analysis, you can identify key gap-closing thrusts required to move the organization forward. Rather than just reorganize everybody into another configuration, consider what you are trying to accomplish.

For example, if a key tactic is to drive quality awareness into all production departments, you might consider eliminating a central quality staff or changing their role in the new organization. If a key strategy is to drive quality compliance so all areas have the same standards, you might strengthen the role of a central quality staff. Form follows function.

Avoid temporary or transitional structures. They are a sign of weak leadership and often lead to confusion. People working in a "temporary" mode are inefficient. Energy is siphoned off as people jockey for position in the final order. You can't be effective in that atmosphere. The leader's role is to push for clarity, fit with the strategic plan, and not wimp out with a mushy transitional structure.

When you change organization structure, the old order will be shaken up. Layers may be eliminated, jobs redesigned. Typically, it is possible to remove about half the layers while simultaneously improving productivity, quality, and delivery. This has a double positive impact, as there are fewer people and each one is more efficient. In addition, many problems associated with communicating down a long organizational chain are reduced. There is less confusion and more clarity of purpose. Although layers are eliminated, there is still need for good people who will perform different functions.

Handled well, this can be an energizing experience, but too often it becomes one of the most traumatic times in the change process. Organizational surgery must be handled delicately because it deals with people's careers. Most managers become defensive if they suspect their level will be eliminated. This natural reaction is a major hurdle, and it has undermined many efforts. Transitions of leadership are particularly sensitive and must be made with care, as I describe later in this chapter. The trick is to continually involve impacted layers, so leaders can make whatever changes are necessary, and yet keep the environment of trust.

A good example occurred in a small, isolated work group in John's Department. He had done some cost benchmarking and needed to make a significant shift to be competitive. He was considering a consolidation of this group with another in a different building. He bounced the idea off the workers and, of course, it was pretty unpopular. Calling all 19 people in the group together, he gave them two weeks to come up with an alternate plan or be consolidated.

John provided a facilitator so the team could meet efficiently to work on the problem. They worked for two weeks while keeping up with production. Finally, they called John and me in at 6 AM one day to report progress. They revealed a plan that, in three months, would improve quality and delivery while reducing the crew size from 19 down to 9 people. They wanted to know if they had our "permission" to do it. I told them it felt like I had just caught the winning touchdown pass in the Management Super Bowl!

They had removed an organization layer and eliminated some straight-day jobs. Everyone had to get additional training and give up some perks they were previously enjoying. In the end, they got down to 10 people rather than 9, but you never saw a more energized and dedicated bunch of people. They *owned* the change.

One key was that John guaranteed people upfront that we would find good jobs for anybody freed up by the exercise. Without that, the result would have been tepid rather than red-hot. Also, without a trained facilitator to help steer them along, things would have degenerated into a kind of an organizational food fight. This is another excellent use of a consultant: to keep people on task. This example demonstrates the power of another vital tool for change: job redesign. In order to remove 9 people, the group had to change the way all jobs were being done.

Redesign Jobs

An empowered team works differently from a conventional workforce. It is important to recast job functions to work well in an empowered state. This means examining the actual work and flow to be consistent with new capabilities.

Job Redesign must be done with care to cash in on the benefit of higher capabilities. The effort is complex because the organization needs to maintain productivity in the old system while new jobs are developed. The key to success is careful planning and execution. Significant retraining will be necessary as people take on new roles.

Having job redesign become part of teambuilding is a good way to ensure proper alignment. This was evident in the above example. If it occurs as a separate exercise, some later retooling is often necessary.

Design Caution: Avoid the BIG REORGANIZATION

The leader can reduce confusion and inappropriate behavior by not making a huge production of a reorganization. This is costly to the organization in lost momentum and needs to be managed as a part of the change process. Too often we see managers advertise a big reorganization as a thing that will save us, and it will be happening over the next 6 months. People don't see the connection between this and the organization goals, so they resist and play all sorts of games, undermining current performance. G. Richard Thoman, President of Xerox Corporation made that mistake in 1998 when he reorganized the field sales force. Not only did it confuse and demoralize the sales people, it also thoroughly alienated Xerox customers. It led to a nearly complete collapse of the corporation and the speedy ouster of Thoman.

The antidote is to view restructuring as a natural part of a process and not a singular event in a vacuum that will sweep in and fix all the problems. When you see people roll their eyes back and say "we're going through another reorganization," it is a good clue the leader is handling it poorly.

Staffing: Selecting the Right People for the Right Job

Selecting people to fill job slots is critical. The right people must be in jobs that make the best use of their talents. Although most groups don't identify people for the slots until after the slots are identified, rest assured everyone is trying to visualize where they will fit. This is unnerving to all but the most secure people. There is no simple cure for this tension but it helps if you are clear about the objectives and sensitive to people's fears. You need to make decisions with strong input from all stakeholders, including support groups, customers, and suppliers. People in the organization need to know their input is valued. Try to avoid a kind of papal succession cloister, where nobody knows what is happening until the smoke goes up.

The design period offers an opportunity for politicking and back-stabbing among the staff. You must set the moral tone to mitigate these natural tendencies. Let everyone know you will not tolerate any inappropriate behavior, and coach people privately if they go astray. In an atmosphere of trust, you will know immediately if people are doing inappropriate things, and you can bring them back to reality gently but firmly.

Often there is an opportunity to go outside for some fresh blood and a more diversified population on the final team. You become a master negotiator, both inside the existing group and outside. Work quickly on these deliberations, because the whole organization is holding its breath for the answer and things are in limbo until people know their roles.

Avoid announcing some of the slots and having several of them with "To Be Announced" as the name. This only heightens the anxiety in the minds of those not yet placed. Make selections with conviction and courage. Do not procrastinate. Sometimes it is necessary to leave a name as TBA if you are negotiating outside for a key resource who can't be freed up. Keep this activity to a minimum, while being sensitive to the need for a timely announcement. It is a balancing act.

Announcing the new organization needs to be done with sensitivity. Some people will have been demoted or removed in the process, others brought on-board or elevated. A one-on-one discussion with all impacted people is mandatory before going public with the results. In these discussions, you can probe for ways to make the announcement more palatable and show sensitivity to impacted people.

When announcing the new structure, make sure everyone gets the message clearly along with the business rationale. Relate the new organization to the strategic plan and the gap closures identified in your SWOT analysis. Make sure all stakeholders get the message. This is often a stumbling block. I recall a very annoyed supplier who was inadvertently left out of the communication in a reorganization. I had to eat a lot of crow before we were on good terms again, and it took longer for this supplier to be comfortable with my personnel selections.

Leaders in Transition

When reorganizing an operation, the most crucial element is selection of the right leaders. Changing incumbent leaders is not a trivial matter.

The transition from a current leader to a new one can be hard on the culture. According to Steven Sample, "Leaders must remember that creating genuine trust is not like dumping instant coffee into hot water. A leader who seeks to operate effectively over the long term needs to minimize turnover among his senior advisors in order to allow trust and candor to develop on a solid foundation."

Make the physical transition to the new leader happen quickly. If the exiting leader has no urgent new assignment, he may argue for a transition period to "bring Sally up to speed on our organization." This is a bad idea from several perspectives:

- The incumbent, Clem, is a lame duck, so his initiatives are in limbo until the new leader, Sally, supports or changes them.
- People relate well to Clem and will seek him out for advice during the transition. This creates loops for Sally to untie later on.
- Usually there is physical space for only one leader. If they are both together for more than a day it becomes pretty awkward to just lock up the office at night.
- Clem and Sally may not have a particularly warm relationship, since she just took his job.
- Clem may be in a grieving process and lack the optimism required to sustain people in transition.
- Sally is in charge, but if Clem is there to "give advice," the signals coming from them will be confusing and muddled.

I recall awkward situations where I nearly had to use a crow bar to get the exiting leader to move out. On the flip side, the most efficient transfer was when I inherited a rather large organization. The exiting leader showed me where the personnel files were, gave me the office keys and his phone number. He indicated he would help me in any way I wanted and then left. The entire transition took less than 10 minutes. That was a blessing, because it started everyone off with a clean slate.

The Adjustment Period

After taking over a new assignment, there is an adjustment period, where the new leader attempts to mesh with the existing culture. Often there is a challenging period where people are unhappy with the new leader, no matter how charismatic. This is particularly true if the previous leader was popular. People go through a grieving process. They are not happy about losing their focus of attention, even though they realize it was a good move for the leader. The typical comment is, "Now we have to start all over and 'train' this new leader. We will lose our momentum, and what if the new person doesn't mesh well with our culture?" The arriving leader has some issues to overcome even before assuming the position.

Normally, the transition process takes a few months. If a group was particularly fond of the previous leader, it could take a year or more, before the new leader is given recognition and full latitude by the subordinates. It is hard to have faith in a new person, when the basis for trust was so entwined with the actions and personality of the previous leader. If they are unhappy about losing the former leader, the actions of the new leader are suspect and there are many "false starts" in the new regime.

In my experience, the average leadership transition is 3-6 months. During that time the new leader finds it difficult to make major changes. Attempts to win people over are often viewed as divisive and awkward. It is a difficult period and everybody is glad when it is over.

Whenever you take over a new leadership position, there will be at least one time when you feel like an ass. It never fails.

Recognize it will happen and get it over with as soon as possible. You can even joke about it to reduce tension. Say, "Well, I guess every new leader makes some mistakes at the start. I'm glad that one is behind us. Let's move on and build from here together."

Except for short-term flexibility assignments, avoid moving leaders too soon. If a leader is moved within a year, people become disheartened. They just completed a transition and have to start over. Ideally, a leader should spend the first year deciding what to do and building trust. The second year is spent developing the team and implementing the new ideas. The third year is living with the consequences of the changes and modifying the course as necessary. Moving a leader before 3 years is inadvisable, and before 1 year, dangerous. It can be done, but expect to do damage control afterward. Note: I am referring to a "year" in a large corporate setting where budgeting and performance measures are annual events. In smaller organizations or high growth situations, the time frame for cycles may be shorter than a year. In these cases try to think in "cycles" rather than "years." The point is, there needs to be incubation and digestion time for change initiatives before leaders are moved.

How will the culture be impacted by a change in leadership? I have made a case that the level of engagement is highly linked to the vision and values of the leader. When a group has developed a pathway toward engagement, what happens when a new leader comes in? Do they start back at square one? The answer is no.

If an engagement initiative is working and trust levels are high, a group can withstand the transition to a new leader more easily. Of course, it is highly dependent on the actions of the new leader. If he comes in and announces that the path we are on is wrong and we must change, there will be pushback. You can expect a long struggle until some kind of equilibrium is reached. If he expresses delight in what the organization is doing, the transition can be nothing more than a speed bump.

The legacy left behind by a departing leader reflects the caliber of leadership. John Maxwell summed it up in "The 21 Irrefutable Laws of Leadership":

> "When all is said and done, your ability as a leader will not be judged by what you achieved personally or even what your team accomplished during your tenure. You will be judged by how well your people and your organization did after you were gone. You will be gauged according to the Law of Legacy. Your lasting value will be measured by succession."

Often the transition to a new leader is less onerous than people anticipate. Reassure people that things will be okay, but avoid talking down to them. I learned that the hard way during a transition of Department Managers in a production area. People really liked their leader, Mark. He had been there two years and was thought to be the best leader they ever had. Mark needed broadening to advance, and another high potential leader, Barbara, needed seasoning as a Manager. When I announced the leadership change from Mark to Barbara, people nearly revolted. In a department meeting to explain my action, I looked out over a sea of angry people. Explaining reasons for the move, I recalled that these same people had been against Mark two years earlier because they had liked the previous boss.

I pointed out that Barbara was very capable and assured them that six months down the line they would like her as much as Mark. This drew a very negative reaction because they were grieving and didn't want to hear it. Ultimately, it played out just as I said. People appreciated Barbara after the transition and, a year later, thanked me for bringing her in. The mistake I made was trying to convince them of this *while they were hurting.* They needed a grieving period. It was important for them to express anger without any pushback from me, and I failed to allow it. Many people feel hurt at the loss of their leader, and adjusting to a new person is scary.

If you are a new leader, your attitude is key to success. Spend the first few weeks listening and learning. It is fine to share personal beliefs with the new group in a "getting to know you" mode, but avoid giving too much early direction. Let the existing team carry the momentum until you know what is going on and have earned credibility.

This does not hold in every case. For example, if you are assigned to lead a group in serious trouble, strong direction may be needed from the very first hour. If you're in the middle of a battle and the previous general has just been shot, there is no time for "getting to know you" activities. You need to direct traffic immediately to stop the bleeding and prevent further loss.

You might take over for a leader who was despised and have to deal with a significant management-to-worker gap. Here it is proper to acknowledge that the previous path was not working. "Let's figure out a better way together" works well in this case.

If handled with care and sensitivity, the transition to a new leader can be smooth with little loss of momentum. The key is to recognize the normal human reactions going on and be sensitive to them. The typical mistake is trying to give directions too soon, before a trust relationship is established.

When upper management considers the chess game of which leader is best in a particular situation, the above issues should be included. It is not just about where the leader is and what is best for that person. Significant leverage can be generated if leadership choices are made with sensitivity to the needs of the organization and the leader. This requires a long-term view.

Create Fluidity and Flexibility in the Organization

Do not view the organization as a static monolith that is the end-all of efficiency for your situation. Bend the structure to meet current situations. If you have an environment of trust and a well-internalized plan, you can shift things around easily. That is a huge advantage over organizations that view structure as something fixed until heaven and earth are moved to change it.

Ken Blanchard tells a story of a Motor Vehicles Bureau in California that illustrates this. He had so many unpleasant memories of long lines and wrong forms that he avoided physical visits at all costs. Finally, when forced to show up in person, he was delighted to see the exact opposite of the stereotype. He got great service and was out with a new license (including a new picture) in 9 minutes. He went to complement the manager, asking how he made the organization work so much better. The manager replied, "My job is to reorganize the Department on a moment to moment basis, depending on citizen need." That attitude changed the whole customer experience from one of dread and horror to adoration.

Thus far, I have concentrated on the perils of leadership transitions and cautioned against too much turmoil. The coin has another side, however, and that is to create learning opportunities for leaders to prevent stagnation. Do this with care because of the pitfalls listed above, but don't ignore it. Use it to keep leaders fresh and challenged.

You might have leaders swap positions for a time. This technique has many interesting advantages and some challenges. Leaders become entrenched in their thinking if they do the same thing too long. Their perspective becomes parochial, no matter how objective their intentions. Assuming the role of another person helps perspective and also keeps groups reporting to both people in balance.

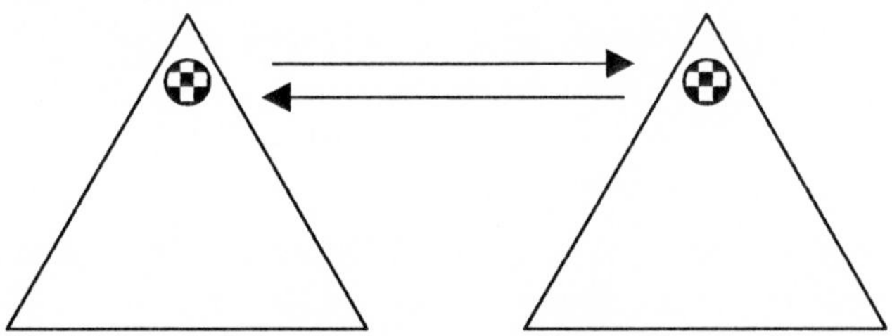

Swapping Leaders

This technique is particularly effective for leaders who are bickering over personnel or turf issues. Sitting in the other person's chair for a year or two helps both leaders see how parochial they were. It is often unpopular with both the leaders and their constituents, so be prepared for some pushback if you propose this. In the end it works extremely well, but it is usually a tough sell.

You can also achieve flexibility by pulling an incumbent leader off for a critical assignment. Let the group be led by someone else in the organization. This allows you to test leadership capability of the substitute in a risk-free way. It also allows the moved leader to get a break and gain new perspective.

Making Personnel Changes

High-octane leaders tend to surround themselves with other good leaders. You can see an interesting dance occur whenever a new leader takes over a situation. There is a shakeout period, where the newly appointed leader gets the new team on-board. Some people have to go. They may not be fired outright, but they need to find another activity in the company or retire. This often happens quickly, within hours or days after a new leader is announced. In the political arena, it happens after every election when the incumbent has lost. Normally, by the time a new administration is in its fourth month, the team has stabilized.

Removing Leaders

In a new leadership position, immediately begin assessing the quality of leaders who now report to you. It is common to change some of the leaders in an organization within the first year after assuming a position. How do you decide who stays and who goes? Simply determine if the current leaders have the ability to take the organization where it needs to go.

There are several evaluation tools that can help. One method is to make a checklist of critical leadership traits and identify how each leader measures up. The information in Appendix A could be used for this, or you could use another listing of leadership criteria.

Most companies have a formal process to evaluate leaders and this is a major source of information. General Electric developed a great process for identifying leaders into 4 categories.

> Type 1 leaders - deliver on commitments while consistently displaying the corporate values. These leaders are always moved forward.

> Type 2 leaders - fail to meet commitments and don't live by the values. These people have to leave the organization.

> Type 3 leaders - fail to make the commitments, but consistently display the values. These leaders are given additional opportunities and training.
>
> Type 4 leaders - make commitments, but do not demonstrate the values. These leaders must be weeded out because they get their results by bullying people or doing unethical things, like cooking the financial books.
>
> (Note: do not confuse this GE leadership terminology with the "Level 5 Leader" as described by Jim Collins in "Good to Great". They are different concepts.)

If you decide to replace a leader, do it with care. This person is in the wrong position and needs to find another job, inside or outside your company, that will allow him to be more successful. As the supervisor, level with the individual; try to preserve personal dignity, and help him find a better fit. Once an incumbent knows he will be moved, his effectiveness plummets, so take action quickly.

This process is difficult, but it can be rewarding. Incumbent leaders rarely volunteer to leave, even if they are struggling or stressed. If they are failing, they believe the situation is correctable over time. If they have problems with values, they are blind to them. It is not a happy discussion to encourage, or demand, a leader get another job. If you are honestly working to help the person, it will show, and the process can be accomplished with grace.

You can provide joy and relief to a person who is in over his head. The difficult case is the person who thinks he is doing well but isn't. If this occurs, it points to a lack of reality and poor communication. Level with the person in a sensitive way to clear the air while maintaining personal dignity.

After removing a leader, I would follow up with the person a year later to see how things were going. In most cases, the person was happier in their new role and grateful to me for the change.

Your ability to outplace marginal leaders in a win-win scenario is highly dependent on your political skills and negotiation skills, along with your personal credibility in the organization. Look for a fit where this person can make a positive contribution as a leader in a different situation or an individual contributor.

Work with other leaders at your level to uncover these opportunities. Create strong alliances with your peers and superiors. Here are several tips that will help you create the right peer-to-peer relationships.

- Treat your peers and superiors with the same respect and integrity as people in your group. Often that is a challenge because you compete with them for critical resources. The best advice is to always use the golden rule.
- Find ways to help them in ways they recognize. Visualize yourself walking around the office with a bundle of olive branches strapped to your back. Each day see how many olive branches you can give away to people who would squabble with you.
- Whenever possible, be a vocal supporter of their positions in meetings. If you act like an ally, it is more difficult for them to view you as an adversary. If you think of them as the enemy, they will reciprocate.
- Go the extra mile to help them solve problems. Sometimes that means taking problem people off their hands to make a fresh start in your organization. It might mean the loan of equipment or other tangible assets. Be bountiful with your assistance.
- Foster great relationships with the key lieutenants of your peers. They have high influence and will help your cause if they see you as a friend.
- Bond with peers whenever possible in social settings. Get to know their families and their hobbies, etc. The closer you are as friends, the more they will help you at work. The basis of politics is that "friends do things for other friends."

- You will negotiate often with peers for resources. Establish a track record of being fair and looking for the win-win opportunities. Never try to win at the other person's expense. It will always boomerang and you will lose in the end.
- Be visible with your concessions. Demonstrate that you deal with fairness.
- Resist the temptation to "blow in" a peer when they mess up. It may feel good at the time but you have made an enemy. You can never afford an enemy if it can be avoided (and it always can.) Some people go around creating enemies to satisfy their ego, their lust for conquest or just to have fun. They don't last very long. If a peer makes a mistake, it's a great opportunity to help them regain equilibrium, not a time to twist the knife. Kindness pays off.
- Do not engage in e-mail battles. If a peer is less than kind in an e-mail, respond to it with courtesy and maturity. Getting into a food fight over some issue has no place in the adult world, yet you see it all the time. Be bigger than that.
- Don't belittle, berate or embarrass people, even if they do things to deserve it. This is a test of your maturity.
- When you make a mistake or create a political faux pas, admit it immediately and ask for forgiveness. Don't try to hide your blunders.

There are hundreds of other ways to foster cooperation among your peers and superiors. They are just common sense and go back to the Lou Holtz advice to "Do what is Right." Note: the above list is not a set of tactics or manipulation of others. Following them shows your level of integrity and moral fiber. Do these things because they are right. Being effective in this arena helps you move people who are in a misfit situation and create slots for new resources in your organization.

As you bring in new people, you demonstrate your values to everyone. The criteria used to evaluate candidates reflects your style. Outstanding leaders put "leadership ability" at the very top of the list when looking for new people. They understand effective leaders have to leverage themselves through other leaders. This is also an opportunity to demonstrate the value you place on diversity.

Ultimately the organizational structure takes shape. It will be fluid with time to be responsive to personal and group needs. The structure must be the enabler of change rather than the product of it. It must allow the emergence of a better and more reinforcing culture.

Chapter 10 - Developing Corporate Culture

An organization where all people are pursuing a common vision in an environment of trust has a sustainable competitive advantage. This chapter will focus on methods to achieve that culture.

What is "culture" in an organization? Webster defines culture as the social structure and intellectual and artistic manifestations that characterize a society. For an organization, "culture" means how people interact, what they believe, and how they create. If you could peel off the roof, you would see the manifestations of the culture in the physical world. The actual culture is more esoteric because it resides in the hearts and minds of the society, in addition to observable behaviors.

Achieving a state where all people are fully engaged is a large undertaking. It requires tremendous focus and leadership to achieve. It cannot be something you do on Tuesday afternoons or when you have special meetings. Describe it as a new way of life rather than a program. You should see evidence of this in every nook and cranny of the organization.

A perfect example occurred in a production department reporting to Diane. With their engagement efforts, people began to feel more ownership of the physical plant. I mentioned earlier that signage and trappings hung on the walls by supervisors often indicate a doomed "program". It is the opposite when workers demonstrate commitment with physical modifications.

The people in Diane's department decided that their scrap room, off a main hallway and visible to passers-by, was an eyesore. After they cleaned it up, it looked like a cleaned-up scrap room but nothing special. The team decided to paint the walls and machines light blue. They had the children of each worker make paper cutouts of stars with messages about where Mommy or

Daddy worked. They hung these stars from strings attached to the ceiling so they looked like dozens of colorful mobiles just overhead. That scrap room was kept scrupulously clean and well lit. There was less scrap to deal with too, because the team figured out how to nearly eliminate it. It became the highlight of every management or customer tour. One look at the room and you knew the people in this area were fully engaged in the business. A key lesson here is that Diane merely set the stage. The ideas and enthusiasm came from the team. You don't have to be in a leadership position to make things happen.

A similar example occurred in a plastic molding production area. For those who haven't seen one, the air is sooty and smelly. The floor is covered with scrap material and there is hydraulic oil leaking from every machine. The machines themselves are dingy and black, so you wouldn't want to touch one. Conveyors are crammed in between machines with little room to walk without tripping.

Now picture a similar plastic molding department run by Jim, where people have taken ownership. The atmosphere is bright and cheerful. The machines are all painted mint green and are spotless. You can nearly eat off the floor and see no signs of leaking oil. The air is fresh and clean, not smoky. There is a large American flag hanging in the center of the operation. Conveyors carry material up overhead so there is plenty of room on the shop floor. Next to each machine is a six foot potted plant like you would find in a hotel lobby. People are obviously proud of the operation and can't wait to show it off to visitors or customers.

Wouldn't you like that kind of ownership in your operation? It is possible if you can create the right climate for trust to grow. A key component is helping people feel special because they are special.

Leaders Create Winners

At work, many people feel forced to endure an unfair world where they feel like losers. In organizations of exceptional leadership, the exact opposite occurs. People enjoy their work because their leader has created a culture of "winners." People become bonded together as a winning team, and joy and celebrations replace the drudgery of work. These are the lucky few that work in organizations where the leader understands how to leverage the small win.

> Jack Stack wrote:
> "Winning is not just a matter of pride, of course. It is also a habit. Unfortunately losing can be a habit as well. When people are in the habit of losing, you won't see fire in their eyes, only sand. If you want to light the fire, you have to begin by creating wins and celebrating wins – by making a big deal out of little victories and then building on the little victories to achieve bigger victories. It's a way of putting fun in the workplace – literally. We throw parties and hold celebrations at the drop of a hat. What we're really doing is creating a team."

Excellent leaders understand a key mission is to create this environment. They know that when they establish a culture of winners, the entire organization will prosper and win.

Success is defined, not in terms of wealth or power, but in doing worthwhile things. There are wealthy and powerful people who are utter failures, just as there are many successful people who have no money or fame. It is the ***journey,*** not the destination, that embodies success. Earl Nightingale in his program, "Lead the Field," identified success as "the pursuit of a worthy goal." Notice it is not ***achieving*** the goal or receiving awards for accomplishing amazing feats. Success is in the doing, in the pursuit. Once you have reached a particular goal, immediately set out a course for the next increment of your life. If this new goal is worthy, the simple pursuit will mean you are successful.

This is wonderful news because you can feel the elation of success every day of your life. It is there in the fiber of your daily living as long as you are pursuing a worthy goal. Teach this insight to everyone in your organization. It will take the drudgery and pressure away, adding joy in its place.

The best way to create winners is to become an expert at positive reinforcement. This is the glue that holds good feelings together and makes a winning culture sustainable. Dr. Ken Blanchard has written more than a dozen books, all focusing on creating this kind of environment. Each one has a new twist to help leaders understand different dimensions of outstanding reinforcement. His teachings have changed the business world over several decades.

Challenges in Creating a Reinforcing Culture

People react positively to effective reinforcement. It is easier to move someone toward improved performance by reinforcing what they do right than punishing them for mistakes. This is well documented in hundreds of books. Though all leaders know the theory, few practice it well. Ken Blanchard's book, "Whale Done" is a simple but powerful book that demonstrates this. In it, Dr. Blanchard provides a simple formula for improving performance:

1. Build trust,
2. Accentuate the positive, and
3. When mistakes occur, redirect the energy.

Determine what motivates people so they don't develop a dependency on having someone notice and comment on everything they do. "The point of good management is to influence people to do the right things when you're not around...Instead of building dependency on others for a reward, you want people to do the right thing because they themselves enjoy it." Dr. Blanchard has demonstrated that reinforcement, if done well, produces spectacular results.

It is sad that many attempts at positive reinforcement actually produce the opposite result. You have probably experienced this yourself, either on the sending or receiving end, and it is very frustrating. Let's examine some of the reasons why positive reinforcement can have a negative impact. I will use personal examples here, but you will recognize the phenomena because you have undoubtedly experienced them too.

Overdone Reinforcement

Ironically, the first example is from a weeklong class on Performance Management. We were studying the power of positive reinforcement and how to achieve it. We were given little buttons or trinkets whenever we did something right or said something profound. At first, it was a unique and refreshing feeling to get something, like a sticker or a pin, for simply contributing to the class. After a few days, the newness wore off and the trinkets lost significance. At the end of the week they became a distraction. They were not reinforcing and the junk was piling up in a bag next to my chair.

At the end, we were given a signed diploma. I have been to many courses and have the diplomas framed in my office, along with academic degrees and awards. This diploma is notably absent. It meant nothing to me and left a bad taste in my mouth. It was put in a drawer somewhere and discarded along the way.

Incredibly, a course to teach the benefits of positive reinforcement had a negative outcome for me. People bristle at the insignificant trinkets spread around in an overdone attempt at positive reinforcement. For some it works, but for many it backfires. Kouzes and Posner write, "You can also trivialize recognition to the point that it is taken for granted and so becomes meaningless or less of a benefit than a right. People lose interest and really never get into the game if a rally cry goes up every time the team simply gets the ball."

Test to see if the tangible R+ mechanisms (positive reinforcements) are perceived as positive or just piling up in a desk drawer. Use a variety of intangible reinforcing techniques, along with the tangible ones, and vary the trinkets you give out. If you always give out stickers, they will quickly lose their meaning to everyone but the die-hard sticker collector. (I have yet to meet one.)

Insincere Reinforcing

Martha was reviewing the performance of her team with her supervisor. Things were going well in some areas, but there were challenges in others. They had a frank discussion, and she got up to leave with several action items. On her way out the door, the supervisor said, "Oh, wait, I forgot. This is for you." He handed her a box and shook her hand. Back at her office she opened the box. It was a clock inscribed, "Thank you for 30 years of dedicated service." Martha told me, "I honestly did not feel anger or pain. It was a kind of a non-event. I still have the clock, but I never look at it and the batteries have gone dead." There is probably a Dilbert cartoon about this somewhere.

I don't mean to tear down the boss. We all have probably done similar things to others unknowingly. We get side-tracked and miss the opportunity for sincere reinforcement. The message here is, look for the opportunities to reinforce and do it with sincerity. A mechanical reinforcement triggered by an HR policy is well intended, but it requires careful execution to have much value.

Not Perceived as Reinforcing

What people find reinforcing is a matter of individual taste. When leaders reinforce using their own frame of reference rather than that of the recipient, it often ends in frustration. For example, many managers instinctively revert to the pizza party as a way to reinforce workers.

Never assume you know what will be reinforcing to another person. Always find a way to test. Your own ideas will often miss the mark.

Jim inherited a technical group. The previous supervisor had a habit of reinforcing perfect attendance by taking people to lunch. Early on, Jim approached a couple technicians who had perfect attendance and congratulated them, asking where they wanted to go for lunch. Sensing by their body language that something was amiss, he discussed the policy. One of them leveled with him. “We never liked those luncheons. They make us feel uncomfortable.” After further discussion, they were delighted to enjoy a day off with their families. If Jim had forced the free lunch, he would have felt good, believing they had been reinforced, but he would have missed the mark.

One year during the holiday season, a business unit servicing the Motion Picture area wanted to reinforce employees for a fantastic year. I got a call from the person organizing the celebration. He had lined up a showing of a first run movie, free for all employees and their families. That sounded great until he said the movie was “Schindler’s List.” I suggested a lighter fare might go better, especially in December with a family. He was resolute and had already obtained a copy of the movie.

I remember feeling physically sick about 1/3 of the way through the movie because of the violence. I whispered to my wife, “I’m not sure I can take this. Maybe we should go.” She was in shock too, but whispered, “Shut up and take your reinforcement!” I’ll never forget how glad we were when the ordeal was over. Driving home, we both had that “deer in the headlight” look on our faces. I said, “I don’t know what we did to deserve that reinforcement, but I hope we never do it again.” Feedback from that fiasco provided the obvious: a family event requires a family theme. The next year, when a similar event was booked, they used “Miracle on 34th Street” and it was much more reinforcing.

A group wanted to reinforce five administrative assistants for completing a Herculean task in record time. They discussed getting flowers or a Mall gift certificate. Someone finally had the bright idea to ask the secretaries what would be reinforcing. They wanted the whole group to take them to a small bistro called “The Crem-de-la-Crem” for high tea. What were the chances of guessing that without asking?

Try giving a couple choices with an open-ended offer to negotiate. For example, as reinforcement for an outstanding year you might offer key people either a family portrait or a weekend away for two. If neither of these ring their chimes, ask if they could suggest another, more appropriate gift. The relative size of what was already offered establishes a framework for choice. People will not try to ante-up the value. If anything, the opposite occurs. They request a more modest gift. The size of the gift has little consequence. You don't need to give someone a Buick for them to feel reinforced.

One supervisor got pretty creative with major gifts. Rather than giving a $200 gift certificate, he would give a DVD Player or a super-putter. Find out something personal and unique about the person, and give something they will use and treasure. Contacting the spouse is a great way to accomplish this. They always know something the person would appreciate, but wouldn't purchase for himself. I found one individual was a woodworker and gave him a couple upscale, engraved, brass and rosewood tools. I know he will never forget the occasion and will think of it often while working in his shop.

Reinforcement Perceived as Unfair

Of all the excuses for not reinforcing well, the issue of fairness spreads out like a nuclear cloud after a bomb blast. Leaders get burnt on this issue once, and it colors reinforcing patterns from then on. If they reinforce Sally publicly, it makes her feel good, but tends to turn off Joe and Mark, who believe they did more than she did. That is why the "employee of the month" concept often backfires. It sets up a kind of implied competition where one person is singled out for attention. That person is perceived to "win" at the expense of others who think they "lose." How do you fight this?

Create a win-win atmosphere rather than win-lose. Focus more on group performance, where the whole group is reinforced with special mention to some key players. Have the employees themselves nominate people singled out for attention. That at least feels better than having the boss "play God," trying to figure out who made the biggest contribution. It's a tricky area. While I mentioned above that you can easily overdo the trinkets, you can never overdo sincere reinforcement. I found the best method is to make reinforcement ubiquitous and continuous.

Developing a Reinforcing Culture

Thus far I have discussed personal reinforcements for a job well done. This is important, but it pales compared with the power of developing a reinforcing culture. That is a social norm that encourages everyone to honestly appreciate each other and say so as often as possible.

Many groups struggle in a kind of hell where people hate and try to undermine one another at every turn. They snipe at each other and "blow people in," just to see them suffer or to get even for some perceived sin done to them. What an awful environment to live and work in, yet it is far too common.

Contrast this with a group that builds each other up and delights in each other's successes. These groups have much more fun. They enjoy interfacing with their comrades at work. They are also about twice as productive! You see them together outside work for social events and there are close family-type relationships in evidence. Hugging is spontaneous.

As a leader, you want to develop this second kind of atmosphere, but how? A good place to start is with yourself. Make sure you are practicing positive reinforcement in a way that others see and recognize. Create an atmosphere where everyone understands and places high value on effective reinforcement. Become a model of reinforcement and praise those in your organization who excel at it. Ken Blanchard has a seminar called "The Power of One" where he emphasizes the incredible leverage of a well-focused individual. As a leader, you invoke that power when you train everyone how to reinforce others by reinforcing them when they do it. It sounds convoluted, but it's really just common sense.

A technique used in my organization was the reinforcement note. Whenever anyone wanted to express appreciation for another, they were encouraged to write a short e-mail about it. The person would address the note to the one that they wanted to praise. I asked for a copy of each one and printed them out. In many cases an "atta-boy" note from me would go back to the person being reinforced. More frequently, I sent a "thank you" note to the person who originated the R+ note praising them for taking the time to write it. During my weekly staff meeting, I would read a selection of the R+ notes from the past week, highlighting any themes. The meeting notes would show every meeting started with these reinforcing activities. This was critical because it sent a signal to everyone in the organization that the culture was more important than the crisis of the day. When you have a winning culture, groups can handle any crisis with grace

Too often leaders become distracted with the immediate crisis and dive right in with the urgent problems of the day. Each problem becomes a stumbling block to trip over. They forget that every day there will be a new dragon to slay and that the culture is what allows elegant resolution to these issues. Spending a few minutes at the start of each meeting reflecting on what is going right makes sure everyone is in top shape with a winning attitude and gives the group the ability to tackle any problem.

We started keeping track of the number of reinforcing notes. The first year we got about 70 notes. By consistently reinforcing this behavior, we got more than 200 notes the second year, and more than 1200 notes the third year. After that, there was no need to keep counting, but each year I was delighted to clean a large stack out of my desk for year-end cleanup. Normally, the stack was more than a foot tall! People at all levels knew their good works were documented and appreciated, often with a public acknowledgement. Further, they felt reinforced for praising others, so the process fed itself, and a culture was developed.

At the same time, we encouraged verbal reinforcement that was not documented. Any time someone saw another person doing something right, they were encouraged to offer praise. Especially important were the "thank you's" any time a person went out of their way to help someone. This caught on like the reinforcing notes and had a powerful impact on the work environment. Making this a reality required that supervisors (and others) reinforce people when they praised their co-workers. As they felt good about doing it, they did it more often.

The key is to create the culture at all levels. It isn't enough for just the boss or a few supervisors to reinforce people. Teach ***everyone*** to do it. That multiplies the impact by however many people you have. As the culture develops, you'll see it spreading to other parts of the organization. People will begin to notice your area is much more positive and productive than before. It will sparkle and upper management will start asking how you did it.

Reinforcement builds confidence in people. Jack Stack, in his book "The Great Game of Business," put it this way:

> "One of a manager's main responsibilities is to build confidence in the organization. To do that, you have to accentuate the positive. If you accentuate the negative, it eats away at the organization. It becomes a demotivator, and management is all about getting people motivated. A manager who doesn't motivate isn't doing his job. You can't motivate if you are continually focusing on the negative."

A reinforcing culture transforms an organization from a "what's wrong" mindset to one of "what's right." The positive energy benefits everyone as the quality of work life is significantly enhanced. In addition, the quality and quantity of work increases dramatically because you have harnessed energy previously lost in bickering and put it into positive work toward the vision. What an uplifting way to increase productivity! ***Instead of beating on people and constantly dwelling on the negative, you'll be generating good feelings and loyalty while you drive productivity to unimaginable heights.*** That is worth doing and easy to accomplish!

Don't get discouraged if you make a mistake in reinforcing. Sometimes you will. It is an area of significant peril, but its power is immense. Continually monitor your success level with reinforcement. Talk about it openly and work to improve the culture. Consider every mistake a learning event for everyone, especially yourself. Often these are comical in nature.

Let your reinforcement be joyous and spontaneous. Let people help you make it special. Reinforcement is the most powerful elixir available to a leader. Don't shy away from it because it's difficult or you've made mistakes in the past; embrace and make love to it.

A hallmark of a true reinforcing culture is that the good feelings are race, age, and gender neutral. As the harmony created by proper reinforcement blossoms, demographic tensions seem to fade. This helps the organization harness the power of diversity.

Creating an Environment that Values Diversity

Diversity has become a mantra for the 21st century. Creating a diverse organization is a key value for most organizations. Some still view it as a holdover from the racial or gender affirmative action programs of the 1970's and '80's. There is often a flavor of "we must do this because it's the right thing to do" in the rhetoric.

Others see it as a trend and pursue it out of social force. There may be a fear factor indicating disadvantaged groups will make trouble if management isn't working on diversity.

There are a multitude of interpretations and programs addressing diversity. Consultants are working to educate people and writing books on it. Some efforts take the form of mandatory training. Eight hours of enforced diversity training for everyone will help raise awareness, but it won't do much to resolve the problems. You must change the underlying culture, which takes significantly more energy.

Diversity issues can be complex and emotional, but there are a few concepts that remove much of the mystery and misery. The objective is to allow individuals to contribute to their maximum potential in an atmosphere that embraces their individuality, rather than represses it.

Think about your own basic needs to insure self-worth. I bet they are as simple and profound as needing to be accepted, included, appreciated, and loved. The real leader is constantly seeking the true essence of others. She works to support and help others live their true essence at work and in the world.

We are all Blind

I can no sooner understand how a pregnant woman feels coming into work than I can eat a slice of the moon. I cannot know what goes on in the mind of the Bosnian refugee who wears the same dress to work every day because that's all she has. The trials of the single black father with a daughter in trouble are impossible for me to comprehend. If you ask me what it feels like to be the first Hispanic CEO in a particular corporation, I haven't a clue. Other people find it equally difficult to understand the forces working within me. That isn't the issue.

Just as people who don't live their values are blissfully unaware of their hypocrisy, so bigots have no clue as well. They cannot see the countless insensitive things they do and say every day. They honestly believe there isn't a prejudiced bone in their body. As W.C. Fields put it, "I am free of all prejudices. I hate everyone equally."

These people see no need to improve their understanding of diversity. Training them is nearly pointless, as they believe this stuff is aimed at others, not them. Start with training aimed at making people more aware. If people open their eyes and admit that, "I guess I do think like a bigot sometimes," (and everybody does) you are making progress. That progress not only helps reduce tensions, it also has a significant benefit for the business.

If our culture truly values the talents and ideas of everyone, we will relate better to customers with our products and services: an external benefit. The organization that draws out the best in each person spends more time pursuing the vision and less time resolving misunderstandings: an internal benefit.

I do not claim to be an expert in diversity. As a WASP, I can't trust my own instincts because they are derived from my own cultural filters and bias. The best environment gives feedback on insensitivity in a way that enables greater understanding.

My leadership team was blessed with a mixture of line managers from a variety of backgrounds, ethnicity, and gender. These were in a constant state of flux because all were growing and moving in their careers, creating slots for others.

Often, it was the minority representation that brought the group up short when we were off base. They would help us realize our gut perspectives were not to be trusted. They would point out when we slipped into a dangerous "group think" or "monoculture" mentality.

In "The Contrarian's Guide to Leadership," Steven Sample described it this way:

> "A highly homogeneous organization is as susceptible to disease and infestations as a large biological monoculture. Every farmer knows that when he and his neighbors plant tens of thousands of contiguous acres in a particular variety of wheat year after year, that variety will soon become vulnerable to new diseases or new strains of insects. Ecosystems that are biologically diverse are much tougher and more resilient in the long run than monocultures, and so it is with organizations that contain a wide variety of people working toward a common goal."

It was important to have these people on the team and critical to listen when they pointed out our naiveté. It kept us growing and searching for a greater appreciation of diversity. Although no group ever fully understands the issue, at least if people are reinforced for pointing out gaffs, you can be a little less blind.

A Reinforcing Culture melts away Demographic Differences

Groups that achieve a reinforcing culture are less preoccupied with diversity. The issue does not come up often because people are concentrating on winning, not demographic equity. That is the way it should be.

You have undoubtedly experienced times of acute awareness of racial or gender stress within your work group. Whether in the minority or the majority, the reality of differences in people is often evident, polarizing words and actions. There is an agenda in the air that takes energy away from pursuit of the vision.

There have been other times when your work group was so successful and having so much fun that physical differences seemed to melt away. You simply viewed teammates as outstanding people. Relationships transcended differences but, at the same time, you were aware of the differences in order to help and support one another.

Imagine if that atmosphere could prevail in your organization. It can. The secret is to develop an organization of trust and love – a reinforcing culture. This environment allows groups to stay on course when issues arise, such as when people take empowerment the wrong way.

Reinforcing can get Tricky in an Empowered Culture

In an empowered organization, people are taking responsibility for things previously done by others. There is a higher level of initiative with increased ownership. This means people sometimes get carried away and do things beyond what management has in mind.

An example might be an operator staying late to clean out a pile of junk on a file cabinet. In the process, he throws away some irreplaceable maintenance manuals that had been left out. The operator's intentions were noble, and he was taking responsibility for his area. However, to the manager, there is a problem. You must reinforce the effort and gently shape the behavior that was in error. If not, people will easily misinterpret it as hypocrisy. In "Whale Done," Dr. Blanchard describes this as "redirecting" energy away from the wrong behavior and refocusing it on things that can be reinforced.

For example, in Dave's area, the shop floor workers had taken over many responsibilities formerly done by managers, including scheduling vacations. During one important production week, too many workers were out for vacation and production schedules were missed. Dave gently coached the teams on the new responsibility of having adequate staff on hand. He redirected energy by reinforcing their willingness to align personal schedules. He handled it with sensitivity, and there was no loss in momentum. If Dave had become enraged and demanded the vacation scheduling be reinstated as a management function, he would have lost a year of progress toward shop floor engagement.

The management layer closest to the shop floor requires the most training and support. The person is usually called a "Supervisor" or "Team Advisor". This level deals with the "us versus them" dichotomy more than any other. The fortunes of the entire organization are made or lost in the trenches of the First Line Supervisor.

Supervisors are bombarded with people issues, while simultaneously being challenged by upper management. Often they are dedicated ex-shop-floor or sales people who have done well and shown organizational ability. They were selected because they got things done and had behaviors consistent with the organization's values. Some had training in leadership, but many were just "appointed" to sink or swim in a new role. Organizations rarely give adequate training and mentoring to these people. They exist and survive as best they can with the day-to-day issues.

If we realize the pivotal importance of these leaders, we will focus on them and lighten the load. Be brilliant in the selection process, and give these individuals the very best in training, mentoring, and support. Reinforce them for their special contributions, rather than load additional sacks of burden onto them like donkeys. This allows more energy to be focused on important things like the outside world.

Opportunities lie with the external market and the customer. The real enemy, the competition, is also external. Unfortunately, in many environments, internal battles consume the most energy. Check out the reality of that statement in your organization. For one day, keep track of how much energy is directed inward at each other, rather than outward. Organizations that rise above the internal fray to focus on the customer and competition have a competitive advantage. Noel Tichy provided an example in his book, "The Leadership Engine." He described the transformation of focus at General Electric that occurred after Jack Welch took over as CEO:

> "In the political arena, Welch took on GE's massive bureaucracy. For decades, GE's 'scientific management' system had been considered one of the company's greatest strengths. It allowed the company to discipline and control its far-flung and diverse businesses. But by the early 1980s, the bureaucracy had taken control, and the company was choking on its nitpicking system of formal reviews and approvals. People were judged and

> paid according to how well they responded to the bureaucratic rules, even though the procedures delayed decisions and often thwarted common sense. Mastering the system had become a stylized art form and a requisite for advancement. The result was that many of GE's best managers devoted far more energy to the internal matters than to their customers. As GEers sometimes expressed it, the company was operating with its face to the CEO and its ass to the customers."

In startup or small companies, entrepreneurial spirit and absence of strata reduce the problem, allowing a focus on winning. Survival is at stake daily, so there is little time for internal squabbling. If an individual does not focus on organization goals, he is expelled with little fanfare. As success leads to growth, the organization takes shape, and the seeds of myopia are sown. Ultimately the large organization emerges with a focus on internal battles and decline begins.

It is possible for large mature organizations to avoid this trap or reverse it, as GE did. It takes outstanding leaders that create an environment of trust at all levels. Good leaders keep the focus on external opportunities by teaching people how to resolve internal problems efficiently.

Develop a Problem-solving Mindset

Many groups flounder or become paralyzed when problems arise. A panic sets in and people lose perspective. Good leaders model sound problem-solving skills. They encourage an atmosphere where logic, rather than emotion, prevails. This is done in a rational and deliberate fashion that keeps people calm.

When facing a problem, put things into perspective first. Give people a chance to vent and voice their concerns. Quickly focus energy on the issue as a challenge to be overcome, rather than a calamity. Keep people from "cause-jumping," assigning a cause before the data is examined. Assemble the right resources based on the nature and severity of the problem. Avoid overkill, but make sure you have enough horsepower and knowledge to understand the problem.

Examine the situation in a logical manner. What are the facts? List observable symptoms and, most importantly, what is not happening that you might expect under these circumstances? This allows you to identify boundaries of the problem. List probable causes in a logical analysis, and begin to eliminate those that do not fit the data. Finally, find a way to test the cause to see if it is the root cause of the problem.

Identifying the root cause as opposed to the immediate cause is critical to obtain a lasting fix. For example, we once had a packaging line that started to nick boxes of product making them unacceptable. Analysis of the problem indicated a push-rod was out of position. It required adjustment.

- Before realigning the rod, we asked why it was out of position. Answer: it had come loose due to a loose setscrew.

- Before replacing the setscrew, we asked why it was loose. Answer: it was vibrating more than usual.

- Before we dampened the vibration, we asked why this was occurring. Answer: it had a very sloppy bearing on a rotating shaft above it.

- Before replacing the bearing, we asked why it was sloppy. Answer: it had no lubrication; it had become dry.

- Before lubricating the bearing, we asked why it was dry. Answer: The technician did not do the preventive maintenance on the machine.

- Before bawling out the technician for not doing his job, we asked why this happened. Answer: Management did not have a good backup policy for vacations, so nobody did his work while he was gone.

After finally reaching ***root cause,*** we were able to put fixes in for all the symptoms in a way that solved the problem for good, and many other problems lurking below the surface were thwarted.

The technique of asking "why" at least 5 times is a good guideline for getting to the root cause of problems. Good leaders keep probing until the root cause is found. This isn't all drudgery, either. In fact, it can be quite comical as most problems, when traced back far enough, become management failures. Seek out opportunities to keep the atmosphere light and enjoyable, even in the midst of tough challenges.

Learn to Have Fun

A hallmark of an empowered state is that people have more fun at work. In the conventional environment, there is little of this. Helping people relax and enjoy the new environment is a part of the deal. There are lots of team celebrations, both inside and outside work. Jack Stack, in "the Great Game of Business" put it this way:

> "You don't need a balance sheet to tell the difference between a healthy company and a sick one. In many cases, it's the difference between going to a ballpark and a funeral home. In a healthy company, you can see and feel the enthusiasm. People nod and smile and look you in the eye. There are often banners around or balloons. Something is always being celebrated – a birthday, an anniversary, a new record, whatever. The bulletin boards are fresh with the latest news. In a sick company, on the other hand, the bulletin boards are filled with announcements required by law – OSHA directives, anti-discrimination regulations, and so on. People don't look at you. They aren't happy to see you. The premises are run down. The stock is disorganized. No one is having fun. Everyone seems depressed. It's as if people are going to a funeral every day, and it may be their company's."

Your organization can develop the ability to have fun while simultaneously improving productivity. Get people involved and let their creative juices take over. For some leaders, this is scary. It seems logical that if people keep their noses to the grindstone most of the time, more output will result. Instead, people get ground down to a bloody pulp and become exhausted and irritable. If there are moments of joy and celebration, people are far more productive over the long haul. The leader needs the wisdom to take a chance and let things happen.

Once a group of employees asked for some money to convert an old storage room into a "multi-cultural center," where people could go to meet or take a break. Conventional wisdom might have said, "Great, all we need is another break room." Instead, I encouraged them and gave them some money (about 60% of what they requested.)

A couple months later, they had a gala opening of the Multi-Cultural Center and it was ***awesome***. The room was tastefully decorated. There were comfortable chairs and a big conference table. No money was spent on the furniture. The employees found it in a surplus area and got permission to use it, along with free trucking for delivery. There was a state-of-the-art sound system with soft ethnic music playing and a video of cultural topics. Around the outside walls were shelves with several hundred precious artifacts the shop floor people had donated from personal collections from their homelands. There were pieces from all over the world, and each one was labeled like in a museum, along with some information on the donor's family background. The lighting was like an art gallery, so the artifacts really jumped out.

This room became a place for celebrations, and the people had proud ownership of it. They, not the janitors, kept it spotless. Once a month, they would have a cultural lunch with a specific country as a theme. People would bring in dishes from that country to share. They rotated exhibits to allow more people to display.

I was proud of them and the room. It became a regular tour stop when top management was in town. They were amazed to see a room organized and managed by production workers, right next door to the packaging lines. When management talked to the workers, it was obvious they were proud of their room and the celebrations it represented.

Productivity also rose during this time. Even with the distraction of planning, constructing, maintaining, and celebrating the room, people felt more connected to the workplace, more engaged in the business, and more productive. They were showing the power of unleashing their maximum discretionary effort.

Unleash your Maximum Discretionary Effort

Most organizations obtain only about 20% of the effort available in the workforce. People believe they are working hard, many complaining about the crushing workload. In reality, nearly all of us habitually operate at a tiny fraction of our capability.

This is not out of sloth; it is a product of the environment. To illustrate this, simply notice the response in times of crisis. An outstanding example was provided immediately following the collapse of the World Trade Center Twin Towers on September 11, 2001. Rescue workers in heavy protective equipment provided heavy physical labor without rest for several consecutive days, attempting to rescue their fallen comrades. If you had tried to get that level of energy the week before the attacks, it would have been literally impossible.

There are countless stories of superhuman deeds performed simply because they had to be done. The old story goes, if you want to find out your real capability in running track, try getting chased by a bear!

There is a difference between adrenaline-induced super human deeds and effort that can be sustained over time without burnout. No one can operate at 100% capacity for long. However, if most of us run at approximately 20%, there are opportunities for improvement. It means we could *double* our output and still be running at less than half our peak capacity. That is worth pursuing. A useful exercise begins with visualization.

At some time in our life, each of us has performed at peak levels. In these instances we were operating at 2-3 times our normal output.

Close your eyes and visualize a few times in your life when this occurred. Take each instance and mentally dwell on it. Ask yourself what was going on. What were you doing and, particularly important, what drove you to perform at that level?

Write down the answer, then move to another example, repeating the same steps.

Once you have several examples, study what you have written. Is there a common theme among them? Look for triggers that evoke superhuman effort in you. Here is a list of typical triggers:

> I felt trusted so I did my best – I wanted to please the boss.
>
> It was literally do or die.
>
> We were "going for it together," and I didn't want to let the team down.
>
> My personal pride was on the line.
>
> I knew what had to be done and I was the only person who could do it.
>
> People needed my help and I gave it willingly.
>
> I was able to earn a huge amount of money in a short time.
>
> I can't stand having things partially done.
>
> The goal was clear and I took up the challenge.
>
> I was afraid that if I didn't get it done, I would be fired.
>
> The whole class was counting on me.

Your reason for peak performance may be the same or different from these. It doesn't matter. The key is to *identify the set of circumstances* that has turned you on in the past. Try to frame this as a short phrase like the ones above.

Burn this thought into your brain because it is your personal prescription for top performance. Imagine the power of this. If someone came up to you with a fortune cookie and gave you a 100% guarantee that written on the paper inside was a phrase that would allow you to double your income while simultaneously enjoying a more vigorous, healthy life would you want to open it? On the paper in front of you is that phrase, except some Chinese soothsayer didn't make it up. You did! It can easily change your life, if you allow it.

Knowing this, you can find ways to trigger it more often; and amplify its impact on your work. Hundreds of times a week, there are opportunities to frame a situation to conform to your "peak performance specification." With a slight change in mindset, your available energy will be two or three times normal. You will perform better, your self-esteem will rise, and people will wonder what's going on.

Look for situations where the elements of your specification are in operation. Volunteer to participate in these, and you will be moving toward your strength. People will notice a change: you have more energy and accomplish more. You are happier and seem to be "in your element" – indeed you *are* in your element.

Translating this to others is tricky because what is a banquet for you may be garbage to me. People's reactions vary.

Top managers did this exercise at a workshop and each had some new insight into what made them tick. The boss described his trigger as, "Parachute me into the jungle with a knife between my teeth." For his underlings, it was more like, "I go the extra mile when I feel trusted and valued." As they shared their specifications for maximum potential, the light bulb went on. No wonder there was great stress in the organization. The top person was leading based on the premise that all people are energized by a jungle survival mentality, but his people wanted clear goals with lots of latitude. Application of this knowledge brought better results and lower stress.

This exercise gives personal insight that allows everyone to ratchet up productivity without pain. It also provides an opportunity for constructive dialog that enhances understanding. The end result is more personal effort and less interlayer stress. It is a very powerful tool.

As you use this technique, keep notes on what works best for you. Practice enhancing your own discretionary effort. Share this with your team and gain further insight through dialog. In other words, ***manage your effort triggers***. You will become fascinated with this and gain much from it.

Once you realize the power of this technique yourself, share it with others. It's a fun exercise for everybody. There is no down side. There is very little investment, and people genuinely appreciate the insight. It has value for them at home and at work. The simple technique can be passed on like a chain letter to people in the community. The only trick is to remember to use this insight whenever possible.

Chapter 11 - Developing People and Teams

The final area of successful change involves building capabilities of people in your organization to match its needs. Focus training efforts on the gap between the current state and your vision. This will ensure the most effective use of training resources and reinforce the organization framework.

Build Capabilities

People have different responsibilities in the new organization. This requires new skills. For most groups, some basic skill training is required by part of the population. Working groups often bring up the need for training in discussions with their leaders. For example, they may recognize a need to reduce conflict if they are to reach the vision. In a trusting environment, they are free to propose some training in this skill. Now this training will have high impact. It is specifically designed to ***fill a known gap,*** and it is championed or ***owned by the people affected***. It is exactly the opposite of a "shotgun" approach brought in by an outsider. Investing in this training is a wise move, as it will move the group toward the vision. As they see their recommended approach working, they will be encouraged to suggest other gap-closing initiatives. You have created momentum toward the vision.

Build Basic Skills

All employees need certain minimum skills to be effective. They must have basic communication skills. Employees must be literate to understand written instructions and write information to be shared with others. For example, employees on the night shift must be able to warn incoming workers, in writing, of a quality issue with a specific machine. They must be able to interpret the spoken language to understand operational or safety instructions. Also, they must be able to express themselves verbally, so others can comprehend. This is especially important in times of crisis or emergencies.

Identifying the basic skills required is a first step. Then comes a delicate process of making those who need the training step forward to get it. Some training will be mandatory and some voluntary. Literacy is a good example. For those who cannot read or write, it is a huge issue. They have built up ways of disguising the missing skills so they can function in the world, albeit at a low level. They are typically embarrassed about the situation and often flatly deny they are deficient. They truly don't realize how many important things they are missing.

Some areas have competency tests, allowing people to demonstrate they are up to standard. This increases volunteers for the training programs. If a person proves deficient in a critical skill, the supervisor works with them to determine training needs. Those who flatly refuse need to look elsewhere for employment.

All employees today need reasonable skill in applied mathematics. They must be able to add, subtract, and deal with fractions or measurements. They must be able to interpret numerical information in tabular or graphical form enough to get the meaning. They need to record numerical production information reliably. All employees should be familiar with computers and be capable of making entries in spreadsheets, invoices, procedures, checklists, etc. They need to interpret data on these forms and not be intimidated by the computer.

All employees need initial basic training on the job they have, and it must be refreshed at some reasonable interval. All procedures need to be understood, especially procedures relating to personal safety and product quality.

All employees should have a good grounding in problem-solving techniques. This will prevent them from making problems worse or creating safety problems by doing the wrong things, like chasing a symptom rather than a root cause.

Leaders are responsible for ensuring that all employees have these basic skills and any others that might be necessary in their situation. Beyond that, there are a number of additional capability areas where a high coverage of employees will pay large dividends to the organization.

Build Understanding of Your Framework

You have crafted a framework for your business including vision, values, mission, behaviors, and a strategic plan. To be effective, these concepts must become part of the culture. All employees need to understand them. Sometimes it takes three or more exposures to this kind of information before it starts to sink in. You need to keep reiterating the message in every forum possible until it becomes embedded into the culture.

Develop Leadership Skills

The more people you have operating as strong leaders, the more successful the venture. Train as many people as possible on the concepts presented in this and other leadership courses. I believe it is important for leaders to teach these concepts themselves, rather than bringing in a professional trainer. Leadership material taught by the person in charge has a high rate of absorption.

Promote the Prevention of Problems

Every problem that does not happen is a major victory for the enterprise. The old adage, "an ounce of prevention is worth a pound of cure," is an understatement. It pays to invest in programs that help people learn problem prevention.

For example, I mentioned earlier in this book that I hate complaints for mixed or misidentified product. They are simply an intolerable failure of the system. We used to call them M&M's. We had a real problem in one production area, where operators were required to make several product changeovers per shift involving dozens of packaging supplies. One wrong supply or an improperly purged packing line on a product change could lead to an M&M complaint.

For some time, we had been getting occasional complaints from customers. I made it clear that the only acceptable number was ZERO. Each time one occurred, we would do a thorough analysis trying to uncover the root cause. Then we would do some "mistake-proof" or "failsafe" changes to the process to prevent that from happening again. We made a huge reduction in the problem, but did not get to zero. There were too many variables and opportunities for something to go wrong, particularly when working around the clock.

We decided to take a preventive rather than reactive approach to the problem. We initiated a program to train every employee on how to spot potential problems. Then we encouraged everyone to report anything that might conceivably lead to a mixed or misidentified product. For example, if they saw a carton from the previous product lying on the floor, that could be a potential M&M.

When an employee reported one of these, they would hand it in and describe it to their supervisor. In return, they were immediately given a bag of M&M candies to eat. Some people didn't want the candy, so they would barter for other things of value with their break room buddies or just give them away.

The program worked like a charm. It got everyone more engaged in looking for possible problems before they occurred and offered a tangible reward as reinforcement. It was also fun. I didn't mind paying for the candy if it would eliminate the problem. Also, as a side benefit, when someone would go into the break room with their bag of M&Ms, there followed natural discussion about the failure and what could have been done to prevent it. These were shop floor people tackling business problems during their personal break time. You don't often see that. As a result, we had month after month with ZERO mixed or misidentified complaints, despite a proliferation of products and packaging supplies.

Teach Statistically Valid Thinking

All professionals and many nonprofessionals should have a course on statistically valid thinking. It is shocking (but understandable) how often people misuse data and allow others to do so. Most people don't realize it. For example, a headline in the Wall Street Journal might read, "Fourth quarter profits at DuPont improved 80% from last year." The implication is that there is a trend. Of course, two data points do not make a trend, and we would need to look at a series of many quarters to identify if there is a real trend. This type of invalid data usage is so ubiquitous that most people are unaware of the distortions. Listen carefully to the advertisements on TV and pick out the misuse of data.

W. Edwards Deming taught that this problem is costly in the workplace. He made the distinction between common cause variation and special cause variation. Common cause variation occurs naturally without any provocation, while special cause is always the result of something specific that happened. According to Deming, when you are asked to explain why something happened, if it is a common cause variation you are simply wasting your time. If you try to fix common cause variation by going after why it occurred, you are stupid. Instead, you should seek to change the system.

In all companies, every day, people are asked to explain why something happened when the observation is a result of common cause variation. For example, let's suppose you are a sales manager for a book company and you plot sales every month on a control chart. Sales typically vary by as much as 15% per month due to common cause and the process is in statistical control. Imagine the reaction if your boss asked you why your sales were down by 10% last month and you responded, "That's an improper question that I am not going to waste my time answering. The sales figures for last month are actually in control and what you noticed was just common cause variation." GULP! You probably would not be employed there very long, yet you would be correct and Deming, if he were still alive, would pat you on the back and pin a medal on your chest.

Imagine that you worked in an area where people were all trained in statistically valid thinking and took it to heart. You would avoid hundreds of wild goose chases trying to explain things that were the result of common cause variation. You would not be trying to invent fixes to problems resulting from simple variation as if they had a special cause. Imagine the time and expense you would be saving your company. That is why as many people as possible should be trained in the right way to analyze and respond to data.

Embrace Lean Concepts

Lean Thinking concepts have been around for about 20 years in Japan. Over the past 5-10 years, they have taken hold in many United States enterprises. This body of knowledge has about 15 different techniques in the tool kit. All are aimed at reducing the many forms of waste (called "muda") in an organization. They work extremely well if applied in an atmosphere of successful change, as we described in Chapter 8. Without that environment, Lean Thinking programs often result in no progress, only confusion. If you start with the right footing and apply the tools consistently without getting discouraged, you can get spectacular results in a very short time. Do not apply Lean Thinking principles unless you have the intention of pursuing these concepts forever. It is a permanent change in your way of operating, rather than a short-term program, even though great results happen rapidly.

Form Effective Teams

People must develop skills required in a team environment, such as conflict resolution, consensus building, efficient team communications, etc. All members must pull their weight with minimal infighting. Team building activities take a multitude of forms, from outdoor experiential workshops, like Pacos River or Project Adventure, to organized in-house training. The latter usually takes the form of a modular approach, where teams experience a series of steps and become high performing teams.

I favor a mixture of classroom activities with outdoor experiential training. This scenario provides significant team building events, while actually working on the items needed for improvement. People spend one hour working on "trustfalls," where actual physical survival depends on good teamwork, then the next hour streamlining the budget or working on a new vision.

These activities are a large investment because the whole team must be included. Typically, groups spend from 5 to 20 days away from the job over a 6-12 month period while learning new skills.

The pathway to highly effective teams is not a straight line. Often groups struggle as they learn new habits and attempt to break down old paradigms. The adage "three steps forward – two steps back" is a common phenomenon in team building efforts. There are periods where negative progress is evident and fortitude is needed. Team members expect things to get better quickly and any setbacks can lead to disillusionment. The leader's attitude during these times is crucial to regaining forward momentum. There must be dedication and constancy of purpose.

Skill of the facilitator is another key to the success. A good consultant knows when to move groups forward and when to retrench. A poor facilitator or a group of trainers that isn't well coordinated can create havoc among the people. This is no place for an amateur. Any consultant or facilitator must fully understand and support the specific values and behaviors of the organization. Make sure you are comfortable with a facilitator before starting any effort. Ideally, the leader will perform a high percentage of the training herself, with a facilitator in a support role. Having the leader do the training is a hallmark of excellent leadership.

Become a Teacher and Mentor

When leading an organization, large or small, you can't do it all. Running the details of a business must be done through others. In large organizations, there might be thousands of others. You need an organization of trusted lieutenants to accomplish the work. To do this, you need to shift your focus from manager to teacher.

The best leaders are those who believe it is their highest calling to personally help develop the leaders who work for them. A large portion of their mindset is spent evaluating, training, and reinforcing leaders under them. The training is not centered on classes or consultant seminars. There will be some of that, but the bulk is personal coaching and mentoring by the leader. The best leaders spend 30-50% of their time trying to enhance the caliber of leaders on their team. Why is this? When you improve the capability of leaders working for you, the whole organization is improved. You are leveraging your leadership.

In my line management role, my job title was Division Manager. I saw my function as "growing leaders." Spending time and energy on that gave a better return than spending time inventing new HR practices or supply chain procedures. John Maxwell, in "The 21 Irrefutable Laws of Leadership," called it the Law of Multiplication. He makes the distinction between developing followers or leaders as:

> "Leaders who develop followers grow their organization only one person at a time. But leaders who develop leaders multiply their growth because for every leader they develop, they also receive all of that leader's followers. Add ten followers to your organization and you have the power of ten people. Add ten leaders to your organization, and you have the power of the ten leaders times all the followers they influence. That's the difference between addition and multiplication."

Develop leaders in as many layers as you have under you. If there are three layers between you and the masses, then develop three layers of leaders. It is not enough to work on the group closest to you. They will get the most attention, simply by proximity and need for interface time. To be effective, you need to work at all leadership levels and make it a personal priority.

Jack Welch is probably the best example of this in industry. At his famous School of Leadership at Crotonville, he was personally involved in mentoring and coaching the thousands of leaders in General Electric. Jack believed that teaching was what he did for a living.

> "It was easy for me to get hooked on Crotonville. I spent an extraordinary amount of my time there. I was in the Pit once or twice a month, for up to four hours at a time. Over the course of 21 years, I had a chance to connect directly with nearly 18,000 GE

> leaders. Going there always rejuvenated me. It was one of the favorite parts of my job."

Do the mentoring and development yourself. Do not hire a consultant to do it. It is fine to have help for certain specific skills, but is a big mistake to let the professional trainers take over. Leadership development must be ***your passion***, one that you take seriously enough to consume a significant part of your time. You don't send people to a one-day seminar and expect them to come out good leaders. The combined snake oil of 100 consultants cannot transform your team into effective leaders as well as you can. Bennis summed it up as follows:

> "True leaders… are not made in a single weekend seminar, as many of the leadership-theory spokespeople claim. I've come to think of that as the microwave theory. Pop in Mr. or Mrs. Average and out pops McLeader in sixty seconds."

Teaching must cover all aspects of leadership. Modeling the way, as well as doing formal training, is the balanced approach that pays off. I always considered leadership training a great way to engage in serious dialog with my team about things that really mattered. I would always come away with new insights. Frequently, it felt like I was receiving more than giving. It is a way to "sharpen your own saw" while you mentor others, a real win-win.

As you use this technique, keep notes on what works best and what you are learning about leadership. Keep a file and develop your own trajectory of leadership. Share this with your team and gain further insight through the dialog. Try different situations and reactions, keeping track of your success. In other words, manage your own leadership progress. You will become fascinated with this and gain much from it.

If you are a young leader, you may not feel qualified to mentor others. My advice is to start as soon as possible anyway. Since this is part of your lifelong pursuit of leadership, the sooner you begin teaching, the more you will know. Teaching is the best way to learn something. I suggest you teach what you already know and seek to learn what you need to know. Don't come across as a know-it-all in your mentoring, especially if you are inexperienced. Rather, ask people to go on an exciting journey with you toward more effective leadership.

In parallel, seek out some good mentors and coaches to help you gain in other ways. Finding a good mentor is important for many reasons:

- A mentor in your organization helps you understand the politics at levels above you.
- A mentor will spread your name in a positive way in higher forums and enhance your reputation.
- A mentor will do damage control if you make errors and show you how to mitigate further damage.
- A mentor will often "pull" you along as she advances in the organization.
- A mentor introduces you to people and assignments that can enhance your background.

Obtaining a good mentor is not as difficult as it seems. Most mature leaders are happy to help out younger talent if they are approached correctly. You let them know how you have admired their style and ask if they can give you some personal coaching. There are two tricks to a successful mentor relationship. First, find a good one, and second, make it a mutually beneficial relationship.

Finding the right mentor is a matter of personal taste, but there are some specific things to look for:

- You need to feel comfortable with this person and vice versa.
- The person must have a reputation as an outstanding leader.
- It is an advantage if your mentor has a broad background. The mentor should know the entire organization and know people in many areas.

- You want your mentor to have "coat tails." Pick a rising star or someone who will be around long enough to help you for the long run. It would be okay to select a mentor close to retirement, but you would be wise to select an additional one who will be around for a while.
- You can have mentors and coaches both inside and outside your organization.
- Often, your boss makes a good mentor, but don't consider this a must. The chemistry needs to be right for a boss to be a mentor.

Interface with your mentor often, but don't be a pest. Be alert to the best ways to communicate with your mentor. This person may find voice mail the best approach, or maybe having lunch every couple months is better. Find out what works for that person and match your approach to that. Make sure you are providing help and coaching for the mentor as well. Your insight can be quite valuable for a senior manager. All leaders need good feedback, and if you have good communication with your mentor, you can easily reverse the role and be a coach yourself. When your mentor feels he is getting high value from a relationship with you, it enriches the dialog and ensures a lasting positive bond.

Finally, set your own course to learn about leadership. Read at least one book per month and attend at least two major seminars on the subject each year. Listen to tapes and CDs as you commute to work and join (or form) study teams among your cohorts. If you choose these wisely, you will have the benefit of the best minds in history. Your theoretical perspective about leadership will be growing, ***along with your practical application of it,*** every day. That combination will quickly shape you into a mature, well respected leader in your organization.

Chapter 12 - The Path Forward

The subject of leadership is so vast, the number of topics is infinite. That is precisely what makes it exciting! Whether you are in a current leadership position or aspire to one, the concepts in this book are important, but only one step in your lifelong pursuit of knowledge. Don't stop here. Accelerate your learning and capability growth, because the fun never ends.

Any organization or group can be great with the right leadership. Whenever you see turned-on people really excited about their work and believing in themselves, a good leader is at work, creating and sustaining that environment. Don't expect some kind of magic wand to wave over problems making everything perfect. That isn't going to happen. A continual stream of problems and challenges provides the food for leadership growth. Enjoy the ride, and train other leaders to see the pleasure in it.

The practice of good leadership takes effort and discipline, but not much more than poor leadership. The key is to establish a real environment that brings out the maximum effort of everybody, while minimizing things that distract from the vision. If you are willing to settle with mediocre performance and get by with tepid leadership, you are among the majority. With very little extra effort but some different behaviors, you can be among the top few percent of leaders in the world. In the process, you will be helping to make your organization great, carving out a future of success in your own career. The choice is yours.

In the preceding pages, we identified the leader's role in making organizations great and described the building blocks that allow everyone to understand what the enterprise is trying to accomplish. You and your team identified values, vision, mission, and behaviors for your business. You learned how to develop a plan with the strategies and tactics necessary to achieve goals based on an analysis of yourself, customers, and competition. This allowed you to communicate a coherent foundation, including your personal passion for the vision, to all stakeholders. You then put that foundation to work as the basis for building an environment of trust in your business.

You were exposed to methods of assessing the caliber of your leadership, along with six key dimensions of leadership: trust, style, communication, strength, outlook, and passion for performance. You saw how these fit into the context of a changing organization. The typical pitfalls inherent in change management programs were discussed, along with positive antidotes for each.

Finally, you saw the change process positioned in the context of organizational design, corporate culture, and developing people and teams. This completed a full view of the theoretical and practical dimensions of great leadership.

If you study and apply the techniques in this book, the quality of your leadership and the success of your organization will be enhanced. The methods work, but they need constant tending to continue working. Leadership is not a one-time thing. It needs to be practiced and refreshed on a daily basis for continuous progress. If you have established an environment of trust, people will let you know when things aren't right and allow corrections so they are always putting maximum effort toward achieving the vision.

Pass your legacy of exceptional leadership skills to future generations by becoming a grower of other leaders. Doing this not only helps the new generation, but it also enhances the performance of your current team. Modeling and teaching outstanding leadership skills is the most effective way to bring your organization to the pinnacle of success and keep it there. You need to make this investment, but it is a joyous one because it enhances the quality of work life for everyone. As a leader, you will have more success, more joy, more followers, and more rewards.

Following these steps means making a giant leap for your organization. At first, it will be a leap of faith for some, but as the momentum picks up you will have champions all over the organization. Outside stakeholders will also notice and appreciate the difference. Customers in particular will wonder what came over your enterprise. It is the perfect way to begin a new relationship with your customers, one that will bring your team more success than they can imagine. The focus of my next book, will be on building trusting relationships with your customers.

There are precious few great leaders in business today. Most don't realize that what they do out of habit or ego prevents them from liberating the power all around them. We need more leaders with the insight to toss the old ways in the dumpster and create a real environment where people are free to be their best. You can be one of the few who really understand what it takes and practice it daily with everyone.

You are cordially invited to join the Leadership Hall of Fame. R.S.V.P.

Appendix A - 16 Critical Skills for Leaders

A basic level and an advanced level are described for each skill area below. This list is intended as an adjunct to, rather than replacement for, conventional leadership skill inventories.

Builds an environment of trust

Basic: Demonstrates consistency of words and actions. Does not play favorites.

Advanced: Recognizes each interface is an opportunity to build or reduce trust in the organization.

Builds a winning and inclusive culture

Basic: Celebrates the "small wins" that lead to overall effectiveness of the team. Draws the best everyone has to offer and does not tolerate exclusion.

Advanced: Emphasizes building culture as a central theme. Understands culture defines the quality of work life for the team. Places high emphasis on this aspect.

Ability to be genuine and connect well with people at all levels

Basic: Communicates at the gut level and frequently tests for understanding. Not aloof or formal, but relaxed and approachable. Meets people frequently on their own turf.

Advanced: Develops mastery for reading body language and uses this to enhance connectivity with all levels. Relates particularly well in group settings or presentations.

Is firm but fair

Basic: Insists that people do what is right. Treats everyone with respect. Avoids playing favorites.

Advanced: Teaches people to police themselves. Requires people to think through situations and make the right calls. Acts as a sounding board or coach, rather than an enforcer.

Leads by example

Basic: Follows the rules and demonstrates full engagement in the business. Calls on everyone to act accordingly.

Advanced: Goes the extra mile to demonstrate passion. Often sacrifices personal gain or comfort to show commitment.

Listens deeply

Basic: Practices active listening and verifies the correct message has been heard.

Advanced: Goes beyond active listening to insure understanding of what is behind the input. Seeks out deep understanding of the issue. Leaves people with a sense of being understood, rather than just heard.

Negotiates and advocates well

Basic: Represents the views of people accurately. Maintains credibility by not overselling the case. Knows when to push and when to back off.

Advanced: Advocates the position consistent with the vision in an empowering way from the employee's point of view. Does not automatically accept bureaucratic hindrances such as "gag rules" without diplomatically pushing back.

Makes good decisions and demonstrates business acumen

Basic: Makes decisions that are consistent with the business direction, but also shows sensitivity to people. Perseveres with good decisions, even when under extreme pressure.

Advanced: Reaches decisions from a holistic view of situations and delegates authority to the appropriate level. Sells difficult or unpopular decisions based on personal credibility and strength.

Builds a reinforcing culture

Basic: Reinforces all behaviors that support the goals. Is unbiased in application of reinforcement. Shows sensitivity to how people view all reinforcement activities, especially the issue of fairness.

Advanced: Tests to verify reinforcement will be viewed by the receiver in the spirit intended before taking action. Verifies reinforcement has the right impact and learns from any miscues.

Communicates well with groups

Basic: Reads audiences well. Avoids the "eyes glaze over" effect by keeping everyone engaged in the topic.

Advanced: Goes beyond the talking/listening aspects and insures the key message is internalized. Verifies understanding of key points before the group adjourns.

Calms stressful conditions and diffuses explosive situations

Basic: Avoids getting into a "mob scene" situation. Contains negative energy and does not allow people to lose control.

Advanced: Deals with issues well before pressure is built up. Allows people to vent, but manages the situation and turns it toward constructive dialog.

Manages personal development

Basic: Seeks input on ways to improve performance. Welcomes constructive input and does not become defensive.

Advanced: Considers the art of effective leadership as a life-long learning opportunity. Becomes a role model of continuous improvement for other leaders.

Generates passion

Basic: Models enthusiasm for the people and the business. Shows personal engagement through actions.

Advanced: Generates passionate engagement in others. Creates a sense of ownership of the business in all people.

Develops others

Basic: Lets people know their development is a high priority. Follows up to ensure all people view their training as highly effective.

Advanced: Seeks to bring out the leadership in all people. Considers all interfaces to be opportunities for growth in capability. Uses current situations as a "living laboratory" of leadership.

Reduces credibility gap between management and first line workers

Basic: Explains policies and seeks out areas for clarification. Makes sure management understands the impact of decisions on people.

Advanced: Communicates effectively in both directions to reduce any disconnects. Negotiates win-win solutions.

Builds a "safe" environment

Basic: Works to create an environment where people feel free to express themselves without fear of retribution. Deals with conflicts in accordance with stated values.

Advanced: Creates an environment of high trust where people are free to express their concerns. Lets people know their input is respected and highly valued.

Appendix B - Abraham Maslow's Hierarchy of Needs

Maslow hypothesized human beings satisfy needs according to a hierarchy. People must have their basic survival needs met before needs on a higher level become important. He defined five levels of need as follows:

1. Basic survival needs such as need to breath, eat, drink, and reproduce
2. Safety needs for protection, comfort, and predictability
3. Need for love, acceptance, and affection
4. Need for self worth, esteem, and personal achievement
5. Self-actualization and the desire for personal growth, self-fulfillment, and the realization of full potential

References

Adams, Scott, *The Dilbert Future*, (Harper Business, 1997)

Barker, Joel, *The Power of Vision,* (I.L.I. Press 1989)

Bennis, Warren, *Managing People is like Herding Cats*, (Executive Excellence Publishing, 1999)

Blanchard, Ken, *Whale Done!*, (Free Press, 2002)

Block, Peter, *The Empowered Manager*, (Jossey-Bass, 1990)

Bolton, Robert *People Skills*, (Simon & Schuster, 1979)

Burns, George, *Gracie, A love story*, (G. K. Hall & Co., 1989)

Byham, William C, *Zapp-The Lightning of Empowerment*, (Harmony Books,1990)

Carnegie, Dale, *The Leader in You*, (Pocket Books 1993)

Collins, Jim, *Good to Great*, (Harper Business, 2001)

Covey, Steven, *Principle Centered Leadership*, (Summit Books, 1991)

Dyer, Wayne, *Manefest Your Destiny*, (Harper Perennial,1997)

Fritz, Robert, *The Path of Least Resistance*, (Ballentine Books 1989)

Goleman, Daniel, *Emotional Intelligence*, (Bantam Books, 1995)

Hitt, William D., *The Leader Manager*, (Batelle Press, 1988)

Iacocca, Lee, *Iacocca*, (Bantam Books 1984)

Katzenbach, Jon R. and Smith, Douglas K., *The Wisdom of Teams*, (Harvard Business School Press, 1993)

Kismaric, Carole and Mikoloycak, Charles, *On Leadership*, (IBM 1974)

Kotter, John P., *Leading Change*, (Harvard Business School Press 1996)

Kouzes, James M. and Posner, Barry Z., *The Leadership Challenge*, (Jossey-Bass,1990)

Maslow, A. H., *Motivation and Personality,* 2nd. Edition, (New York: Harper & Row, 1970)

Maxwell, John C., *The 21 Irrefutable Laws of Leadership,* (Nelson, 1991)

Morgan, Gareth, *Imagin-i-zation*, (Berrett, Koehler, 1997)

Nierenberg, Gerald I. And Calero, Henry H, *How to Read a Person Like a Book*, (Pocket Books 1971)

Nightengale, Earl, *Lead the Field*, (Nightengale Conant, 1986)

Oakley, Ed and Krug, Doug, *Enlightened Leadership*, (Fireside,1991)

Peters, Tom, *The Pursuit of WOW!*, (Vintage, 1994)

Powell, Colin, *Primer on Leadership* - presentation.

Sample, Steven B, *The Contrarian's Guide to Leadership*, (Jossey-Bass,2002)

Senge, Peter M., *The Fifth Discipline*, (Doubleday 1990)

Stack, Jack, *the Great Game of Business*, (Currency Doubleday 1992)

Tichy, Noel M. *The Leadership Engine*, (Harper Business, 1997)

Welch, Jack, *jack:Straight from the gut*, (Warner Business Books, 2001)

Wellins, Byham & Wilson, *Empowered Teams,* (Jossey-Bass, 1991)

Zigler, Zig, *Top Performance*, (Berkley 1987)

Order more copies of this book!

Order through your local bookstore, or online at Amazon.com.

Wholesale orders may be made through Ingram's or Baker & Taylor.

A Leadership Partnering Corporation

Leadergrow offers ***unique and more effective leadership training*** than other programs because:

- Training is customized to fit your needs exactly rather than a "shotgun" approach or a "canned" program
- The content has higher impact. Decades of corporate leadership experience are fused with deep academic study and research.
- Training is personal, focused on usable knowledge rather than abstract theory. What you learn today you apply today.
- Content is all meat and no filler. Learn more in less time. Classes are lively and experiential, focusing on dialog, not lecture.

Training covers over 100 skill areas critical to outstanding leadership. Each is tied to a central theme: creating an environment of TRUST. In this atmosphere, improvement efforts so critical to your business do not backfire or stall, but charge ahead with confidence. With Leadergrow training, untested leaders learn new effective methods while those with more experience are energized to get skills out of the toolbox into daily action.

Maximum flexibility to fit your needs with perfection.
Leadergrow material is not a survey course or predetermined program. Modular concepts that fit your unique situation can be assembled quickly ***at no cost*** into a program laser-focused on your needs. Before training, you work with us to determine the unique level, timing and content for each situation. The result is convenient, affordable, customized training with high impact.

Contact : For more information write Robert Whipple at bwhipple@leadergrow.com Telephone: 585-392-7763
Website: http://www.leadergrow.com

Printed in the United States
1145600005B/79-609